Bramley's Home Front

A Surrey Village During World War II

First published in Great Britain in 2007 by
Bramley History Society
Bramley
Surrey
UK

www.bramleyhistorysociety.org.uk

Compiled by Evelyn Hodgson and Evelyn Nash, assisted by Russell Hudson
and Hazel Mulkeirins

Typeset and design by Eric Hill

Cover picture - ARP Wardens & Messenger Boys
courtesy of Geoffrey Knapp and Michael Grant

ISBN 978-0-9528401-1-4

CONTENTS

Introduction 4

The Beginning 5

Evacuees 8

Rationing & Shortages 13

Civil Defence & Other Volunteers 20

Work 31

Everyday Life 37

Schools...48

Military Presence 55

Aerial Activity 62

Train Bombing 67

Those Remembered 75

The Austere Peace 78

Acknowledgements 86

Index...88

INTRODUCTION

The village of Bramley lies on the A281 three miles south of Guildford in Surrey. In the 1931 census its population was 2023, and it was then part of Hambledon Rural District.

2005 saw the sixtieth anniversary of the end of WWII

In tune with the general national commemorations, Bramley History Society mounted an exhibition at the Bramley Fête. A great deal of work was done by committee members, gathering memories, and copying newspaper and official publications, to preserve details of those people left at home to cope with shortages, restrictions and the dangers of the Blitz and later bombings while the younger men went away to fight.

It seemed a waste of effort that all this work should be just stored away in the archives, and so the idea of this book was born.

If ever there was a civilians' war, this was it

The rise of air power since World War I brought, not just news of death and destruction, but the actualities right into our village. This book attempts to give a picture of civilian life in Bramley during and after World War II. 'The Home Front' was a Government slogan.

Inevitably, with over 80 people interviewed, it has been possible only to use extracts in this book, but all the full transcripts of peoples' memories are stored in the Bramley History Society archives.

There are many books about World War II that run from 1939 to 1945, but this booklet is only partly chronological. It starts with the outbreak of war, and ends with the peace, but in between memories are generally given under subject matter, and so overlap.

Memories are fallible, and we have received varying versions of events. Wherever possible, checks have been made with official records.

THE BEGINNING

War was declared on 3rd September 1939 and contingency plans which had already been made everywhere because of the threat of war began to be implemented. The Government was poised to control food supplies, transport, and put air raid precautions in place. In August the Royal Navy had been mobilised, and other Reservists called up.

Unlike some, Bramley seems to have been really organised from the very beginning.

At Bramley C. of E. School Mr Brown, the Headmaster, called a special staff meeting on 13th July 1939 to 'consider arrangements for protection in case of war', and on 24th he attended a meeting at Capt. Adgey-Edgar's (billeting officer) on the subject of children's evacuation. That same day, instruction commenced in the care and fitting of gas masks. Many were found to fit badly. On 2nd August a final gas mask drill and fitting was held before the holidays.

Surrey Advertiser

2nd September 1939

Ready for Emergency

On Thursday it was learned that billeting arrangements had been made at Bramley and that the ARP (Air Raid Precautions) work generally was regarded as efficient. Street lamps had not been lighted during the week and Special Constables were carrying out certain duties. The Red Cross First Aid Post at the Village Hall was ready to come into immediate use should the necessity arise, and was open day and night.

A few memories of Sunday, 3rd September 1939

Bernard Hill

We were in the choir for the 11 am morning service in Wonersh Church. The Vicar, the Rev. L. A. Brown, announced to the congregation the news that war had been declared. We then sang 'Oh God our help in ages past', and the Vicar closed the service. Returning home the air raid siren sounded. The local Air Raid Warden from the nearby shop in Eastwood Road, resplendent in his uniform and steel helmet, was mounted on a bicycle sounding a wooden rattle as he traversed the road, warning of an imminent gas attack. This caused instant fear as one struggled to put on the newly acquired gas mask. I remember my mother having great difficulty putting my three-year-old brother Geoff into his rubber container. To our relief the warden soon re-appeared, this time blowing a whistle. This was to indicate that the gas attack was over and it was safe to remove one's gas mask.

Michael Grant

My mother, brother and I heard the announcement where we were staying at Shoreham-by-Sea. We returned home to find my father had already made a dugout in the garden.

Dorothy Lee

It was a very hot summer and my cousin from Birmingham was staying with us. My brother Jim, my cousin and I were sitting on the sofa. When the warning siren, which was at Luxford's Garage near us, went off, we all put our gas masks on immediately.

Joint memory of Doug Realff and Gladys Lucas

Doug and Gladys were 19 and 20. Their families were next-door neighbours in Birtley Rise, and after hearing the announcement of war, met out in the back gardens.

The young people didn't really take in the implications of the event, but their parents plainly did. Mrs Napleton was crying, as she was French, and her family lived at Amiens, near the German border; Mrs Realff cried too. Later they all had a drink together.

Phoney War

Once war was declared, everything and nothing happened. Nationally the period of the Phoney War set in when, although the troops went to France, the expected air raids and gas attacks did not occur; but on a personal and village level there were sudden, disruptive and frightening changes. Evacuees arrived, signposts and place names were removed, most milestones buried, and the Blackout came in. Whilst the Parish Council minutes don't mention the war until June 1940, there was much organisation of voluntary work, air raid precautions and general civil defence work. The following summary from the School Log Book gives a vivid picture of the turmoil in the village.

Mr Brown was recalled from holiday on 24th July to prepare for the evacuation of London children, which began on 1st September, with the school being used as a reception/billeting centre. Mr Brown and the London teachers had the difficult task of putting two schools into one, but by the 11th, children were back at school, the village children in the mornings and the evacuees in the afternoons. Mr Brown had to organise all teaching materials for the London school.

A constant stream of supply teachers came and went and often Mrs Brown stepped in to teach. On 6th December there is a cry of despair from Mr Brown about the constant calls on his time, both in and out of School, by unscholastic activities, evacuees, Air Raid Precaution measures and village social events. 'It is not possible to relegate such outside questions to out-of-school time because.... I have no private life.'

The Blackout was a shock, street lamps were switched off, no light was permitted to be shown from buildings and vehicle lights screened from above. The cost of blackout material was a heavy expense for poorer people and sometimes-homemade shutters were fitted. Church bells were silenced, to be rung only in the event of invasion.

Barbara Gall

I remember the blackout and if a crack of light showed through the watchman would come and tell us off. This did not really apply to us as we only had an oil lamp downstairs, and used candles in the bedrooms.

Other major changes

Snowdenham Hall, Unsted Park and Bramley Park were all requisitioned by the Army and the Royal Surrey County Convalescent Home was moved from Worthing to Bramley Manor.

Identity Cards

Identity cards were issued in 1939 to all civilians recorded on the National Register. They were carried by everyone from 1939 until 1952. There was a need for complete manpower control made difficult through mobilisation and mass evacuation. Cards were used mainly with a ration book so that civilians could claim their allowances of food and other goods.

NATIONAL REGISTRATION IDENTITY CARD

War Reserve Police Force

Bramley Wartime Police

During the war many police officers were on active service in the armed forces, leaving the constabulary staffed by older men. To fill this gap the War Reserve Police was set up. Many retired men and those from reserved occupations were recruited as special constables. As well as the usual duties of keeping law and order, they were responsible for setting off the sirens, issuing gas masks and seeing that they were correctly fitted and carried at all times. They also worked closely with the Civil Defence workers and patrolled the streets during the blackout.

Freda Carpenter and her brother Ray Stevens remember their father dressed in his uniform ready for duty after his daytime job. Betty Brockman's father Alf Stevens was also a Special Constable, as well as working night shifts.

EVACUEES

Captain Adgey-Edgar was the Head Billeting Officer for Bramley when the evacuees started coming to Bramley, one of seventeen dispersal areas set up in the villages surrounding Guildford. It was organised so that each centre was expected to receive parties at two hourly intervals. The Women's Voluntary Service (WVS) arranged tea and buns and Bramley School was closed temporarily and used as a reception centre, the village hall was used as a first aid post. Householders volunteered to take the evacuees into their homes, for which they were paid a small sum. Extra blankets, camp beds and mattresses were provided where necessary.

People loaned their cars and drove the evacuees to their destinations. A depot was opened in Bramley High Street for the receipt of articles of clothing, especially boots, three times a week. Many of the evacuees came from Wandsworth or Croydon.

Villagers' Memories

Joan Dunn

I had a girl cousin, aged seven, who lived in Gravesend. As the war progressed, her parents sent her to stay for safety in Bramley with us. My parents also were asked to take a couple of evacuees, so they went to the village hall and collected a brother and sister from Clapham. My father was delighted to have a boy in the home. However the girl shared a room with my cousin and told her rather starkly the facts of life – to my aunt's dismay. In the end the two children went to stay with the Edgars. During their stay neither their parents nor anybody else made any attempt to contact them. When they came they only had the clothes they stood up in. They had to have clothing and shoes provided for them by my parents.

Dorothy Lee

We had several lots of evacuees staying with us. My mother used to make them clothes. She was particularly fond of a little Irish brother and sister called Benny and Maureen from London, pictured opposite with us. The night they left Bramley to return to London there was a particularly big air raid, and as we never heard from them again, we wondered if they had been killed.

Joan Grant

I remember Stanley Ede and his brother Cyril, they were evacuated from London, and stayed at Eastwater House. Stanley drowned in the swimming area in the river at Wonersh Bridge. He was buried in Bramley Cemetery. All the children from the school had to stand in the Bramley Cemetery lining the path from the gate to the chapel and sing a hymn.

Freda Carpenter

My mother had a ten-day-old baby and three other children. She was asked to take an evacuee, Duncan Mackenzie. He became like one of the family, and stayed with us till he went into the Navy. We still keep in close touch.

Angela Harms

We had a spare bedroom in our house and we were able to take two evacuees from London. The youngest was called Norman, aged about six. He cried a lot and did not settle. His mother took him back to London. The other boy Roy Fitt was about seven years old. He settled well and stayed for the duration of the war. He attended Bramley School where he passed his eleven plus examination, and then went to Godalming Grammar School. His parents visited frequently and brought the family lovely boxes of chocolates. He later went to Magdalen College Oxford. He kept in touch until he died a few years ago.

Olive McEntee

When war started we were asked to take in some evacuees from London. We only had two bedrooms and had to make our small sitting room into a bedroom. Our evacuees were Mrs Seale, her daughter Betty, and son Patrick. I slept downstairs with my sister Janet and Betty Seale. Mrs Seale had our old bedroom and Patrick slept in her room. Mrs Seale had an older daughter Rita; she lived separately and was very unhappy where she was living. After a while my mum said, "Let her come to live with us", so a single bed was squeezed into our room for Rita. We all got on very well together and when my mum took a job driving Elwin's bread van Mrs Seale looked after my sister and myself.

Patrick was a very mischievous little boy. He was afraid of the dark and one night took a box of matches to bed with him and managed to set fire to his bed. He shut our cat in a drawer in the bedroom and when we found her she was covered in face powder. He also put a button up his nose and it got stuck there. Rita, the eldest girl used to climb out of the bedroom window to meet her Canadian boyfriend without her mother knowing. She used to bring us back sweets to bribe us not to tell her. After the war my parents kept in touch with the Seales until they died.

Guy Selby-Lowndes

At the Vicarage we had two schoolmasters from the London school billeted on us, Mr Wadsworth and Mr Burt; the latter subsequently joined RAF. They shared a large bedroom which previously I had shared with my brother Greville. As he was in the Army and my sister Rachel in the RAF Nursing Service there was plenty of room.

Reminiscences of Evacuees

Leslie Banks

In 1939 my mother and four of her children, including myself, were evacuated to a village near Petersfield. My elder brother Bill, being almost fourteen and just about to start work, stayed in London with my dad. In early 1940 no bombs had fallen on London and my mum and dad wanting to be together again so we all went back. In September 1940 the bombing started again; by this time our sister was almost old enough to work. Myself and brother Ronnie were evacuated with the school to Dorset. All with our luggage labels on our coats plus our gas masks, small suitcase and small toy. While we were living there our parents William and Violet, sister Sylvia and small brother Derek were killed by a direct hit on an air raid shelter. Our elder brother Bill was saved because he was out with his mates and took shelter elsewhere. When all this happened our lives simply lost direction, we had been just trying to keep going until we could go home again and now we were cast adrift. Ronnie started to behave badly and was sent to live on a farm where the people were very good to him and he became very happy with them after a while. I was sent back to London to my granny. When the bombing got too much we would dodge off to friends of hers in the outer suburbs for six weeks or so. Then back to London when it grew quieter again. I lost count of the number of schools I went to.

Then my Gran became ill and I was sent to Bramley. A social worker brought me to live with Mr and Mrs Archie Hill at Hurst Hill Cottages, Birtley Road. They treated me as their own child. Everything that they could do to help me feel happy and secure they did. They were paid a small amount for my keep but this hardly fed me. They bought me clothes and shoes, Christmas and birthday presents. After the War I continued to live with Mr and Mrs Hill, did my National Service and spent my leaves with them. I brought my future wife Dulcie to meet them as though they were my parents. I lived with them until I married in 1953.

Roy Hibbs

In 1940 I came to Bramley. My first recollection was meeting with Mrs Campbell at Summerpool House. I found her a charming and active lady who at the time we met was chipping cement from used bricks for re-use on another garden wall. Mrs Campbell asked me questions about my family and details about my life to date. Luckily she took to me and I was eventually integrated into the household. My duties were to be a companion and helpmate to Edith the maid. I became a washer-upper and an expert potato peeler. I usually had meals in the kitchen with Edith - when she was away I ate in the nursery with Mr and Mrs Campbell's two children, Jennifer and Primrose, along with their governess, a young Spanish woman. I found Mr Campbell a quiet, serious gentleman. We got on quite well. I believe he appreciated the help I gave him in the garden. During school holidays I got myself an early morning paper round for the newspaper and bookshop at Bramley Railway Station.

On reaching the age of fourteen in October 1941 I left Bramley and Summerpool House to start my working life in London. I am enormously indebted to Mr and Mrs Campbell for showing me the side of life I would never have known, and I will always be eternally grateful.

Duncan Mackenzie

I was eight in 1939, and lived with my family in Croydon. In September 1939 our school was evacuated to Brighton. My mother came with my elder brother and me, as my sister was a baby.

During summer of 1940, with the war perilously close to the coast, it was decided to move all children away. The following period is a little hazy. I remember boarding coaches, and then we seemed to be driving for ever, and we had no idea where we were going. We had become separated from my mother and most of our teachers. Then I remember driving down a lane with high sandy banks (I later knew this was Iron Lane). We eventually arrived at Bramley Village Hall. After some swopping around, my brother and I were billeted with Mr and Mrs Skinner in Eastwood Road, with my mother and sister again nearby. In 1941 my mother moved to Dover to be with my father, and I went to the Stevens family at 21 Hurst Hill Cottages. There was already one evacuee there, and four Stevens children still at home. How we all survived in such a small house heavens knows – but we did. Mrs Stevens (Auntie Ivy) had a new baby, but managed somehow.

Looking back, I became more and more one of the family. Life settled down into a routine of mornings free (when we explored the area) and school in the afternoons. Some time in 1942 we remaining evacuees were amalgamated with the village children, and full time education became a reality. Village children and evacuees all got on well together. There was no distinction, we were all Bramley children.

On 1944 the doodlebugs arrived. There was no time to go to the shelters, so children got under desks. Mr Chapple (Headmaster) and I used to stand in the playground, and when we heard a doodlebug, I was sent running through the school, blowing a whistle.

My career after leaving school included the Royal Navy, the Police Force and Social Services. I have remained in close touch with my wartime family in Bramley all through the years

Many families made their own evacuation arrangements

Ray and Nita Oliver (now Hart)

Ray (10) and Nita ((8) were brought up from Portsmouth on the 1st September 1939 by their Naval farmer to live with an old aunt and Uncle, Mr and Mrs Vokes, in Brewery Cottages.

It was a shock for them, two town children who had never seen the country. They did not know their relations well, and the cottage had no electricity. They went to school with the evacuees, but made friends with village children. Nita remembers always being cold and hungry.

They stayed for four years. When Ray left school Nita went home with him. Ralph Durrant kept in touch, and fifty years after the war, he and Pat Jackson organised a reunion in the Wheatsheaf for them and villagers who had known them. Nancy Smith also keeps in touch.

The photograph shows Ray and Nita, with their little brother John and their father in Bramley.

John Ives

My mother was a Bramley girl, but we were living in Chessington and my father was in the RAF. Every night we went into a shelter with the neighbours, we were so squashed together we could not lie down and I slept with my head on a broom. Because of this we came down to my grandmother's cottage in Woodrough Lane because of all the bombing near home. I was eleven, Audrey and Brian younger. I remember our first night in Bramley vividly – bombs fell in the Park.

I didn't think much of that. That first night, too, we three children had to share one single bed – Brian and I one way, Audrey head-to-tail with us. After that things got sorted out, but when my father or uncles came home on leave, I would go and spend the night at Gordon Hedger's house nearby. Bramley was already a very familiar place and being with all the family things didn't feel all that different. Because my mother had been a Bramley resident we were judged as locals and went to school with the village children. When there was rivalry with the official evacuees we naturally sided with Bramley children. All three of us still live locally.

Keith Bothamley

With my grandmother I came to Bramley in early 1940 when I was six. We lived with my grandmother's brother, Walter Hogsden, and his wife, on Gosden Common. At Kenley we lived in Valley Road, just below the aerodrome, and my parents felt it was too close for comfort. I wasn't bothered about leaving my parents as I had my Nan and had often visited Uncle Walter, Auntie Rose and the cousins at the Nursery, so it was all very familiar. After a while our house in Kenley was badly damaged and my parents rented a house in Station Road. My father joined the Home Guard and commuted to Lloyds in London from Bramley Station.

St. Catherine's School also had evacuees

Précis from a school magazine

In autumn, 1940, Miss Symes, Headmistress of St. Catherine's School, was asked to take in eighty girls from St. Mary's Hall, Brighton. She really had no spare room to house them, but agreed. In the event only thirty girls came and everyone settled down to live amicably together.

Several Dutch girls attended St Catherine's School; their families were evacuated from Holland with the Philips Company which occupied Snowdenham Hall from 1940 to 1948. They went back to Holland after the war.

Summary from an article in St Catherine's School Newsletter

Autumn 2006

Erika Werner was a German Jew, her father had been dismissed from his job in 1937 and she was expelled from school. In May 1939 she was sent to England and admitted to St Catherine's School. Two months later she returned to Holland for the summer holidays but the outbreak of war prevented her return. Her parents had managed to escape to Chile, but it was only in January 1940 that an uncle finally succeeded in arranging her return to England.

The school offered her refuge and she continued to live there throughout the war. Apart from finishing her education, she took a secretarial course in Guildford, did war work in a local factory, and worked at the School. From late 1943 she served in the ATS.

Her uncle and many other relatives died in the concentration camps, but when the war ended she joined her parents in Chile.

Always grateful for the School's hospitality during the war years, Erika returned on a visit in 2006.

RATIONING & SHORTAGES

Petrol was rationed in late September 1939, and was according to delivery or work needs. Many private cars were sold or laid up on bricks in storage 'for the duration'.

Food Ration Books were issued in January 1940, and continued until well after the peace.

Amounts varied thorough the war, but the basic weekly allowance in 1940 was:-

Bacon and Ham	4 oz (115g)	Butter	2 oz (57g)
Sugar	8 oz (230g)	Cheese	1 oz (28g)
Tea	2 oz (57g)	Margarine	4 oz (115g)
Meat	1s 10d (9p)	Cooking fats	2 oz (57g)

The meat ration was in money to give a choice of cheap or expensive cuts.

The Points system of 16 points per month, later increased to 20, gave people options: -

Luncheon Meat	16	Cereals	4
Sardines	16	Rice, Sago, Tapioca	2
Canned fruit	8	Dried peas, lentils	2
Baked beans	4	Dried fruits	8
Condensed milk	8	Biscuits	4
Dried egg	1 packet per week		

Expectant mothers and babies had special allowances of orange juice and cod liver oil, and children had their own ration books. After many complaints, an extra cheese allowance was given for all manual labourers.

Poultry, rabbits and fish were not rationed. Jam and marmalade were rationed in March 1941; clothes in June 1941; soap in February 1942; sweets and chocolate in 1942

Bananas vanished, oranges were reserved for very small children and expectant mothers. Whale meat was introduced; it was not rationed, but was universally rejected and used as dog food. There were many shortages and queuing became a wearisome part of many women's lives.

Lilian Hampshire

I was isolated at Thorncombe, but at least all the tradesmen still delivered. My rations and milk came from the Co-op in Godalming. Bread came from Mr Botting's bakery at Hascombe, coal from Lees, of Godalming. My young children had cod liver oil, which they hated, and rose hip syrup as a supplement.

Ingenious substitutes, barter and welcome gifts helped eke out the frugal rations

Avis Day

The day the Canadian Black Watch arrived one lad came to our cottage for water for his truck. Mother made a pot of tea and was rewarded with a case of evaporated milk. She was so afraid she would be accused of black market, so under the bed went the case and each tin used was flattened and buried.

Beryl Freeman

If a consignment of oranges came into the shops they were saved for the young children. I remember my half brother Francis getting them and I would swap my sweet tokens with him for an orange.

*" It may be a long held ambition, but you
can't have a smallholding in here"*

Cartoon from The Smallholding by Basil Blythman

Ula Oakley

In Eastwood Road we had a shop opposite us. An awful lot of people could not afford to pay for the food they had coupons for. My mother used to buy up the extra food and give the boarders at St Catherine's a good tea!

Joan Dunn

Some people made cakes with liquid paraffin as fats were rationed. I was given a slice, unknowingly, and couldn't tell any difference – the maker watched my face anxiously as I ate! My father raised some young cockerels one year and I carried them into work, feathers and all, on the bus. The recipients had to deal with feathering and drawing them. I remember the horrible smell from the potato and vegetable peelings boiling to feed the chickens.

Dick Turrell

We did not go short with me working on a farm and growing our own produce. Every Sunday morning we used to take out the ferrets and go rabbitting. I used to love rabbit stew.

Jean Hopwood

We kept chickens and ducks in the garden, but the fox got the ducks! Instead of our ration of eggs, we had a ration of grain to feed the chickens on, otherwise they ate potato peelings. Because we had dogs we were able to get tripe, which was not rationed, from the local butcher. I remember cutting up the Daily Telegraph for loo paper.

Fred Waller

My family rented the farmhouse at Brooklands Farm, though the land was farmed by Mr. Yendle of Cranleigh. Food was quite easy at the farm during the war, we grew vegetables and used swedes and kale from the fields. Our father caught pheasants and rabbits. On Sundays he and his mates would have a pigeon shoot, and often got 50 to 60 birds. My sisters worked as Land Girls at Rydinghurst, so we got extra milk as well. We also had a massive orchard with all sorts of fruit.

Betty Brockman

I remember what I wore on my first day at work -- a Scotch kilt, a jumper, my school shoes and white socks. I had a navy blue reefer coat, too. Nobody pulled my leg. The first coat I bought, in October or November that year, was dusky pink. I bought it in White's, and had to give 18 coupons up. You got 20, twice a year. Lisle stocking were one and half coupons, but fully-fashioned stocking were three, shoes were five.

Lilian Hampshire

I couldn't afford to use our clothing coupons, but usually managed to exchange them for things we needed with family or friends. I also did a lot of 'make do and mend', turning garments, cutting down clothes for the children. I did knitting and made rag rugs from scraps of material and it was only recently I got rid of the needles and hooks.

Joan Dunn

You couldn't get stockings till later, when the Yanks came, so we used to rub gravy browning into our legs and get a friend or sister to draw a seam down the back and hope to goodness it wouldn't rain!

I had a white wedding in 1942. We bought lace for my and three bridesmaids' dresses from John Lewis in London. For some reason lace wasn't on coupons; we had to give up coupons for long slips underneath, of course.

Government assisted food schemes

British Restaurants

Joan Dunn

The Ministry of Food established British Restaurants, places you could eat cheaply and quite well. I used the one in Upper High Street, Guildford, as the Tax Office wasn't far away. We were only too glad to get any food that wasn't on ration.

Avis Day

We had no canteen so usually we took a packed lunch or occasionally lunched at the British Restaurant in Godalming. Lunch consisted of greasy mince, over boiled cabbage, smash potatoes, and watery gravy. We preferred having cheese on toast at Stovolds Farm Dairy.

Jam Making
The late Irene Elliott

Reprint from 'Surrey Within living Memory'
Surrey Federation of Women's Institutes 1992

In wartime the WI was ready and willing to organise help wherever needed. Our biggest job was the jam-making scheme. Much fruit was being wasted in the countryside when sugar rationing limited home preservation, so W.I.'s founded jam making centres. The Ministry of Food issued sugar; local people provided fruit and cooking-know-how.

Our little WI at Grafham and Smithbrook made a ton of jam and not one pound was rejected by the Ministry Inspector, who then took it away to the national store. So don't let anyone get away with sneering at jam and Jerusalem.

Grafham & Smithbrook WI 1946

Surrey Advertiser
24th October 1942

The fruit preservation centre is now closed after a very successful season in which 1,066lb of jam and between 70lb and 80lb of chutney and pickles have been made and disposed of, Mrs Dickinson, secretary, reported.

Rural Pie Scheme

Joan Grant

I remember the "pie shop". The WVS sold pies in the derelict shop opposite the butchers, they were made at Bernards Shop in Guildford.

Evelyn Nash

My mother used to go down to the village to collect our allocation of the meat pies. These were very welcome, hot or cold.

Parish Magazine
July 1946
Ministry of Food Rural Pie Scheme.

Meat pies and sausages will be on sale at the Village Hall every Friday 10 am – 12 noon. Under the scheme the Ministry of Food issue fats, flour and meat to cook, to enable people in country areas to provide extra meals without coupons.

Dig for Victory!

A huge campaign encouraged everyone to grow as much of their own produce as possible. Many villagers had from necessity always grown their own vegetables, but others, urged on by the 'Dig for Victory' advertisements, dug up lawns and flowerbeds. Many an Anderson shelter had a fine crop of marrows on top. More people than ever kept chickens.

Robin Hill

In 1938/9 all the gardens on the river side of Eastwood Road terminated at the top of the eastern canal bank - and were fenced off from it. Many residents had made gated openings in the fences so that they could tip garden refuse in the old canal bed, but none had attempted enclosure - we were the first to do so. Early in the war we dug up all the lawns to plant vegetables and in about 1940 we were the first to exploit the canal by clearing the bank down to the remaining central ditch to plant potatoes. I do recall that at the time there was a visit by someone we took to be a bailiff - but I think my father convinced him that our efforts were necessary in wartime.

The village school helped too

Parish Magazine
April 1944
E.J.Chapple

Another way in which progress has been made is the development of the school garden. This has been turned over to wartime food production and though we still have a wonderful sample of weeds we have produced about a ton of tomatoes, a ton of potatoes, a few thousand lettuce and a ton of swedes, and various odd vegetables.

The money for the produce has considerably swollen our school funds, which now stands at £100 – collected during the last fifteen months.

Unofficial food sources

People with big gardens or chickens often managed some useful informal bartering, but no one has mentioned black market goods. Many a surreptitious joint of pork came through the 'Keep a Pig' scheme to folk who had not officially given up their bacon ration towards it. Many villagers also supplemented their food rations by feeding off the land. Rabbits and pheasants were plentiful and not always obtained legally and poaching was commonplace.

Evelyn Nash

My mother, having fruit, vegetables and plants from the Nursery to barter, seemed to do quite well with her Guildford Market connections. We ate pork produced by stallholders from Worplesdon, and sometimes got extra sweets from a nearby shop. The clothing materials were definitely black market though; based on the amount of fabric purchased, she paid 2s.6d. (12p) extra per coupon.

Do's and "Don'ts" — THE WAR-TIME ABC

―――――― By "HOUSEWIFE" ――――――

DON'TS, do's, and dishes that you have discovered yourself and proved successful are the hints and recipes that win prizes in the Victory A B C.

Write your hint or recipe—it may have to do with cooking, food, furniture, or any household problem—on a postcard. See that it begins with the letter D and keep it short, with your name and address at foot. Send to "Housewife," "The People," Acre House, Long Acre, W.C.2, to arrive not later than May 24.

Half a guinea is awarded to the sender of each one published. Here are last week's prizewinners:—

CHEAP AND CRISP

WHEN frying fish or fritters use ¼ lb. of plain flour and ½ a teaspoonful of bicarbonate of soda. Sieve together and mix with water to a smooth batter.—Mrs. Robson, 11, Lancaster-gdns., Southend-on-Sea, Essex.

CHAMPION "APPLE" SAUCE

PEEL rhubarb and cut in pieces. Put in saucepan, add 2 tablespoonfuls of sugar. Boil, then mash. Serve with roast pork.—Mrs. R. Fulluck, 9, Whitby-grove, Swindon, Wilts.

COTTON REELS

COTTON REELS nailed to kitchen walls make useful pegs on which to hang towels, etc. They do not rust or tear articles as nails do. Paint to match walls.—M C Ladigo, Llantilio, Crossenny Abergavenny, Mon.

CHEESE HINT

WHEN cooking cheese add a little flour. It will not be stringy, but more creamy for eating.—Mrs Baker, 1, Cecil-rd., Stretford near Manchester.

CHOCOLATE DESSERT

SOAK overnight 4 tablespoonfuls oatmeal in ¼ pint household milk. Cook slowly until oatmeal is soft, then add 1 tablespoonful sugar and 1 dessertspoonful cocoa, and cook slowly for ¼ hour. Add a few drops of vanilla flavouring and stir well. Pour into a wetted mould to set.—Mrs. Slater, Seafield-st., Cullen, Banffshire.

COTTON SAVING

IF, when sewing on buttons, you put a piece of protective muslin, removed from Elastoplast first aid dressings, at the back of button, it will stay on much longer.—Miss Pendall, Main-st., Hockwold, near Thetford.

CLOVE TEA

CLOVES, added when making a pot of tea, greatly improve the flavour. Drop two into teapot, according to taste.—Mrs. M. Kirkpatrick, 46, Mottingham-rd., Mottingham, S.E.9.

PATTERN SERVICE

No. 778.—LITTLE GIRL'S FROCK

BOTH frock and knickers are included in this little girl's summer outfit. Both easy-to-make designs. Instructions how to remake from larger garments also included. Sizes to be had, 2-4, 4-6 and 5-8 years. Size 4-6 years (frock and knickers) takes 2½ yds. 36-in. material.

Paper pattern No. 778, with diagram and full instructions for making up is obtainable from "The People" Paper Pattern Service, "Colintraive," Southcote road, Reading, Berks., price 1s. 6d. POST FREE. Cross postal orders /& Co./. State No. 778 and size required. Name and address in BLOCK LETTERS. Please retain sketch for reference.

CIVIL DEFENCE & OTHER VOLUNTEERS

Bramley was just south of the GHQ defence line, General Headquarters Anti-Tank Line, running the length of the North Downs, which included many pillboxes built near the rivers Tillingbourne and Wey. On 1st January 1939 The Air Raid Precautions Act came into being and local authorities had to set up systems. On 14th May 1940 Anthony Eden, then War Secretary, appealed for men between the ages of seventeen and sixty five not engaged in military service to enrol for the Local Defence Volunteers. The Fire Service was re-organised, air raid systems put into place and air raid shelters dug. Other agencies such as the Red Cross and the Womens Voluntary Service backed them up, all ready should there be an invasion.

ARP Wardens

The duties of an Air Raid Warden included: ensuring that the blackout was observed, sounding air raid sirens, ensuring that people went into public air raid shelters in an orderly fashion, checking gas masks, evacuating areas around unexploded bombs, helping to rescue casualties from bomb damaged properties, finding accommodation for people who had been bombed out, judging the extent and type of damage and informing the Control Centre to send out the rescue services.

Geoffrey Knapp was an ARP Messenger boy

The leader was Captain Fargus. Besides the adults there were five or six young boys in the troup. We wore black trousers and jackets and black berets. We also had helmets with CD on them. In the event of an invasion our job was to carry messages for the Home Guard or the army. We had to go on foot or on our bikes without being detected by the enemy. We had to know all the back ways and bolt holes around Bramley and in the surrounding villages. We sometimes did exercises with the Home Guard, the Canadian soldiers taking the part of the enemy.

Once two of us had to take a message to Guildford. We knew that the 'enemy' was holding the Crossroads at the Grange. When we got almost to the stream we crossed the road to see if we could spot them. We were ready to turn into the church and jump over the back wall if any soldiers popped out of hiding.

We saw no one so we jumped on to our bikes and raced past the Grange as fast as possible. We then rode on to Guildford without incident. When we came back Captain Fargus asked how we had managed to be so quick. We were too embarrassed to tell him we had just slipped through, so we said we went behind the High Street houses and into Chinthurst Lane. Captain Fargus said there was no way through there, but there was. We had gone that way many times before.

The ARP Wardens walked up and down the three main streets of Bramley which were Birtley Road, Eastwood Road and Snowdenham Lane. People were told in no uncertain terms if any light showed from their house. Anyone who continued to ignore warnings was fined. Gladys Gill at Grafham was an Air Raid Warden out at night walking from Nore Lane to the Leathern Bottle to see the curtains were always shut, but she said no light could ever be seen. Joan Goodwin was an ARP warden for the Highways Department. She had no uniform and wore her riding breeches and blue overalls. She had no formal training and could be called out at any time to do anything.

Arthur Dunn

My father, living in Drodges Close, was a Warden and patrolled Eastwood Road every evening without fail. The one night he decided not to go out, incendiary bombs fell on the lower part of the road; dad was furious. Some people had to be evacuated from their houses for a while and old Joe Barnard, Phil Tickner's father, said 'It's the first evening out me and the Missus has had for years.'

Robin Hill

Like all children then we walked to and from school, which entailed turning from Station Road through Hall Road which was the epicentre of the war effort. Here the ARP had erected corrugated iron buildings, one used for fire practice fighting petrol blazes with stirrup pumps and the other for gas mask practice with tear gas. (This area is now Windrush Close)

Air raid shelters and sirens

Basil Blythman

I remember walking down the lane at the side of the foundry. Suddenly the siren went off! Being daytime I thought that the country was being invaded, but it was a false alarm.

Beryl Freeman

The shelter at the MHH factory was previously a pit used when the site was a tannery. They had reinforced the roof, but a lot of water got into it in the winter.

Gladys Lucas

My father set out to make a shelter. A neighbour asked him what he was planting, and he replied "Onions". In fact it was an extremely well made shelter, shared with the Realffs. Electricity was laid on, there were bunks on each side, and each family had its own flight of steps to go down to it.

Nancy Smith

My father built a shelter in the garden, which was only ever used to store potatoes in. My mother said "If we have to die, we'll all go together."

John Hodgson

My family were living at 'Long Acre' on the Horsham Road. My father and our neighbour Mr Lyons decided to build a shelter in the Lyons' garden. However they had not reckoned with the high water table, and it flooded. The next attempt, supervised by our gardener, Mr Wheeler, a World War I veteran, was built in our own garden. This shelter was used regularly. The warnings usually went off about eight o'clock and we would go there for the night, until this shelter too eventually became flooded. My father then prepared a room of the house with loose bricks where the window had been, so if we had to make a hasty exit from the house we could just push the bricks out. Every now and again, incendiary bombs were unloaded by the Luftwaffe. Two landed in the front garden and two in the back, but no damage was done to the house.

Ray Stevens

Sixty eight years ago when I was five, we moved to Chestnut Way. When the war started we built an air raid shelter in the back garden. It eventually collapsed, and there is still an old chair buried there.

Gladys Gill

We did not have any air raid shelter, my family sat under tables or on seats round the fireplace hoping it would save us if we were hit by a bomb.

Ena Baldock a schoolgirl at Lord Wandsworth School, Gosden Common

The V1s and V2s were a regular feature of our lives and we were given trousers and a coat to put on every night when the siren went, we then went to the shelters which I believe were alongside the laundry. We spent most nights there, laid out like sardines in a row of mattresses that felt damp, one row on the bottom one row on the top. The junior girls were on the bottom and every time somebody turned over up top our eyes were showered in rust. One night we were just leaving the building to go to the shelter when the tail light of a V1 went out, we have never moved so quick, rushing to the safety of the shelter.

Surrey Advertiser
Electric warning systems
18th October 1939

Bramley now has three electric air-raid systems in place, which it is hoped will adequately cover the well-populated part of the Parish. These were provided by public subscription. They were installed by Messrs Troughton and Young of Knightsbridge, London, now at Birtley House, Bramley, who not only generously subscribed but also wired these sirens free of charge. The head warden wishes to thank all those who subscribed towards these sirens. (These were placed at the Wharf, Luxford's Garage Birtley Rd, and at Bramley Fire Station off the High Street.)

Gas Masks

There was fear that the Germans would use mustard gas, and gas masks were provided for every citizen.

Surrey Advertiser
29th March 1941

The Head Warden of Bramley, Capt. F.N. Fargus R.N. desires it be known that a gas chamber is being set up at Woodrough (by kind permission of Mrs Feeney-Hyde) where the public will be able to test their respirators. The days when the gas chamber will be open will be announced later.

Hazel Mulkeirins

I was four and a half so was issued with a standard black one, a smaller version of the adult mask. Toddlers had a red rubber mask with two eyeholes and a flappy rubber nose. This was supposed to be less frightening for them. A baby had a kind of small rubber carrycot, which had a transparent cover which went over the top and zipped round and sealed tightly. I think the mother had to operate a pump by hand. We had to practice getting our masks on in double quick time against the time when we might really need them. Gas masks had to be carried about wherever you went. At school we had to put them under our desks and wear them round our shoulders at playtime. The masks were issued in a stout cardboard box with a cord attached for slinging over the shoulder. After some time new filters were delivered to be fitted to our masks. This involved unscrewing the round metal breathing apparatus and screwing on the new one.

We then had to have our masks tested. A summons was sent out to everyone to go to Woodrough House (pictured left). Mothers with school children were to go after school. That was us. Our names were taken and we waited our turn. While we waited, the fit on all the childrens' masks were checked to see that we had not outgrown them. The gas chamber looked like a large, long shed with no windows and big doors at both ends. At last our turn came. In went the mothers carrying the toddlers and babies. In went our mother and my brother Guy and me, hand in hand. My heart was pounding; Tear gas was then pumped in from cylinders outside. We saw and felt nothing. My dad had fitted our filters correctly and our masks fitted well. Some were not so lucky and had sore eyes afterwards. They had new filters fitted by the men doing the testing and had to go in again.

The Home Guard

The 5th Battalion of the Surrey Home Guard

The Local Defence Volunteers were soon renamed the 'Home Guard' and it was made compulsory for men not in uniform or in reserved occupations to join.

The four basic duties were:

1) Reporting information to the authorities.

2) Delaying and obstructing the enemy as long as possible.

3) Protecting vital points, railway properties, telephone exchanges and reservoirs.

4) They were to have a good local knowledge so they could act as guides to the regular army if required.

At first they were only issued with an armband and later denim uniform. This was later replaced by a serge army uniform. Many villagers remember their fathers in Home Guard uniform.

G Company at St Catherine's School when they disbanded in December 1944

Doug Realff

When the Bramley LDV was formed I attended their very first meeting at The Bramley Grange Hotel mews. About fourteen of us turned up. There were three youngsters and the rest were old boys, veterans of the 1914-18 war. There were no designations and we were given an armband with LDV on it to wear on our right arm. Our weapons consisted of pitchforks, a twelve bore gun and a four-ten.

We were sent out to look for Germans coming down on parachutes. We continued to meet at the Bramley Grange Mews and did two nights a week on duty. There were never more than eight of us; we did four hours on and two hours off. One night a week we had to guard a railway bridge at Peasmarsh. When we were not on guard duty we used to sit in the gatehouse to the Vulcanised Fibres Factory at Shalford. The older men were given five rounds of ammunition for guard duty. We sat on empty oil drums on which planks were placed for seats around a table with a hurricane lamp. One night we were sitting there, two men went out, being careful not to let any light show on the outside and two men came in. No sooner had they both sat down opposite me, when suddenly there was an almighty bang, the light in the hurricane lamp went out and the hut filled with blue smoke. We then started hunting for the bullet and found it embedded in the brickwork above my right shoulder.

David Hooper

My father was too old to be called up but as a former Territorial Army Major, he joined the Local Defence Volunteers and subsequently the Home Guard and commanded G Company of the 5th Battalion of the Surrey Home Guard. His CO was Lt Col Hopewell who was my housemaster at Cranleigh School.

Jim Hook

At the beginning of the war I joined the local Home Guard. We used to meet at St Catherine's School and do exercises on Chinthurst Hill. I was only in it until 1940, at that time we had no uniforms or guns. Jack Grant of Tanyard Cottages was in charge.

Gradually more men became involved, the LDV became the Home Guard. In Surrey it was divided into twelve or thirteen battalions. In July 1940 the local LDV became the 5th Battalion Surrey Home Guard.

The 5th Battalion was divided into eight companies. These covered a large area of South West Surrey.

B Company

(Shalford, Chilworth, Blackheath, Albury, Farley Green, Wonersh and Shamley Green)

Russell Hudson

I remember that my father was in B Company as he wore an armband with B on it. He had a motorbike and I think he may have been a messenger for the Shalford Company. [Records show that Headquarters B Company were at Ashleigh House, Shalford.] I think my father went up to Eastwater House on occasions and I remember his tunic hanging up in the cupboard under the stairs for many years after the war.

In the years when our Country

was in mortal danger

Gilbert Sydney HUDSON

who served 28 August 1940 – 31 December 1944,

gave generously of his time and

powers to make himself ready

for her defence by force of arms

and with his life if need be.

George R.I

THE HOME GUARD

G Company

(Bramley, Grafham, Busbridge and the south west environs of Godalming)

The Company was divided into Platoons, most Bramley men were in 64 Platoon, their headquarters were in the Green Room next to the stage at St Catherine's School.

64 Platoon G Company

Michael Grant

When Anthony Eden gave his broadcast asking for local Defence volunteers my father, Theodore John Grant, who fought in the Great War, got on his bicycle and cycled to Guildford. There were four

people in the queue in front of him, so he was the fifth person to register in this area. He came home with a tin hat, gas mask and a LDV armband. My father was a Platoon Commander for the Bramley Platoon. Our front room became their armoury. We had a World War 1 Lee Enfield, sticky bombs and grenades. Churchill had appealed for weapons and some of the local gentry donated some beautiful guns. There was a Winchester 2.2 Repeater. When father had gone to work we used to fire it outside, and then clean it up again so he would not know that we had used it. There was a Browning Automatic which we could just about hold, we put a target on an old oak tree at MHH and shot at it.

John Grant

My father encouraged me and several friends to join the Home Guard when I was 16. I remember Reg Pullinger; we were full members, uniforms, tin hats, rifles etc. and did guard duties. We were allowed

take our rifles home without ammunition. Live ammunition was issued for use on the firing range. We had our headquarters at the back of the hall at St. Catherine's School, and had use of the kitchens. Miss Symes, the headmistress was very pleased to have the Home Guard at the school on duty every night of the year. I joined the Army when I was seventeen and the Home Guard membership counted towards my war service.

BRAMLEY,
Surrey.

Feb. 25th, 1944.

TO WHOM IT MAY CONCERN.

This is to certify that No.14443371. Pte.J.H.Grant was enrolled as a member of No.64 Platoon. 'G' Company 5th Bn. Surrey Home Guard on Sept. 1st, 1942. and continued to serve with this Unit until Feb.10th, 1944.

Signed. T.J.Grant H.
O.C. 64 Platoon. 'G' Company.
5th Bn. SURREY HOME GUARD.

Dorothy Lee

My father had one arm shorter than the other and was very disappointed when the Army found him unfit for active service. He joined the local Home Guard and he used to do lookout duties at Chinthurst Hill Tower. Once he came back from rifle practice at Bisley with his elbows grazed and bleeding from lying on coconut matting whilst shooting. My mother, who was a very good dressmaker, helped out by altering the standard regulation uniforms to fit the men better.

Hazel Mulkeirins

My father had seen service at the tail end of the First World War and was made a Quarter Master Sergeant for the Bramley Platoon, right from the start. He had to give orders to some men who were privates, who had previously been his customers. He kept his pistol in the sitting room underneath the armchair, his rifle fitted under the sofa. (He kept his ammunition in the same room too). When our mum was out of the way my brother Guy and I would sneak into the sitting room, where we were forbidden to go, and finger them. He was out at least once or twice a week. Sometimes there were weekend manoeuvres, he went on church parades, and he learned to shoot at Bisley.

In the Home Guard my dad learnt to make a Molotov cocktail. He showed us children how to make one. First you found a stout bottle which you put petrol in, you left plenty of room at the top for the vapour to build up. Then you stuffed a long cotton rag as a wick leaving it sticking out of the top, put on the stopper. You then lit the wick, gripped the neck of the bottle and threw it against something hard. The idea was that it exploded on impact. We know that this happened because we children tried making one.

John Brown

My grandfather, Jack Brown, was in the Bramley Home Guard. He had a Browning 303 rifle, when he died we found ten rounds of ammunition in his bedroom.

65 Platoon G Company

Cecily Taylor

Women were admitted to the Home Guard in April 1943 and myself and my work colleague Jean Stewart, who had been evacuated to Shamley Green, decided to join the Home Guard. We and six or so other people (from Godalming area) joined the Signals section of the 5th Battalion. The Lieutenant in charge had a wireless shop in Godalming. We met once a week after work. Our headquarters was the Oast House at Gate Street. Here we learned how to use the Morse Code. Besides this I remember only having one target practice and a lecture at Unsted Park by Colonel Beauvary. We had no uniform and wore a plastic badge covered in gold with the letters HG on it. We were an isolated group, and only met other sections at the final parade.

66 Platoon G Company

John Mackney

My family moved to Peasmarsh from Portsmouth to escape the bombing. My father volunteered to serve as an Air Raid Warden and I as a messenger in the Civil Defence. In 1942 when I was fifteen I joined the Home Guard. The Peasmarsh Platoon was officially known as No 66 Platoon G Company, 5th Battalion Surrey Home Guard. We paraded three times a week in Peasmarsh village hall or on outside exercises.

On the fourth Sunday in each month we went to the rifle range opposite Rice's Corner, to fire Sten and Bren guns and occasionally throw practice grenades. On every eighth night we marched from Peasmarsh to the Company headquarters located at Lee Farm in Bramley, to stand guard overnight and to march back the following morning. Our officers were Capt. Holford, who ran a building firm in Guildford and Lieut. Cuter, a nurseryman from Artington. There were about twenty one men in the platoon and the only names I can remember were Sgts Kingshott and Garnett-Harper and Privates Poore and Plaw.

There were about twenty one of us in the platoon. When I was sixteen I joined the Post Office Telephone department and because of this I was told by Captain Holford to take the men two at a time to the local telephone kiosk to instruct them on how to use a telephone. War exercises were held against the Canadians who were based locally.

Godalming and Farncombe Rifle Club

G Company 5th Battalion Home Guard held a meeting at the Church Hall Bramley on 11th January 1945 for the purpose of forming a rifle club. Their first shoot was in March 1945. This became the Godalming and Farncombe Rifle Club by Bramley Golf Club, which still exists at Foxburrow Hill Road today.

Fire Fighting

At the outbreak of war the Government were worried about the Luftwaffe dropping incendiary bombs and causing fires. Some 86,000 stirrup pumps and tin hats were issued to Air Raid Wardens and local authorities.

The Government established the Auxiliary Fire Service. People who had normal jobs during the day could now be compelled to fire watch for a maximum of forty-eight hours a week. The local fire brigades trained them and they were known as Supplementary Fire Parties.

At one time the Parish Council considered having a board made for damming up the stream should the water mains get damaged by enemy action. Youngsters helped out, for example, Arthur Brockman was a messenger for the fire service.

Surrey Advertiser
Anti-bomb demonstration
27th Jan 1940 (Wonersh)

Incendiary bombs will be used in demonstration of methods of combating them in which the Public will be invited to take part which is to be given by the Local Auxiliary Fire Service at 7.15pm on the Common at Wonersh on Wednesday next, and on the Green at Shamley Green the following Wednesday.

Basil Blythman

There was a fire engine which towed the pumps kept near the Foundry and Brewery Cottages. My father became an Auxiliary Fireman and could be called at any time. He had a black serge uniform like the regular firemen. I remember he took the Bramley Fire engine up to London to help out during the Blitz.

Throughout the village, areas were issued with a couple of tin hats and a stirrup pump.

Barbara Gall

My father was a firewatcher in Snowdenham Lane, I remember him wearing his tin hat.

Georgina Harvey

I remember that we had a stirrup pump in Eastwood Road and took it in turns to fire watch.

Dorothy Lee

In Birtley Road my family kept the stirrup pump and had the letters SP painted on the gatepost to indicate its presence.

Owners of factories and large buildings were responsible for providing firewatchers. At MHH three workers took their turns weekdays, and four people did firewatching over the weekends.

Joan Dunn

We often stayed on at the Guildford Tax office, working overtime. Often the sirens went in the early evening, or it was our turn to firewatch. We had camp beds in the office. I'd often come off firewatching at about 7 am cycle home for a proper wash and breakfast, and cycle straight back to work.

Other voluntary agencies which supported the Civil Defence Forces

The Red Cross

When war was declared the British Red Cross and the Order of St. John joined forces to form the Joint War Organisation. County branches of the Red Cross organised units called Voluntary Aid Detachments (VAD) who were trained in first aid. When the evacuees came a First Aid Post was set up by the Red Cross in the village hall. The Rev. Selby-Lowndes was the Bramley Commandant.

Charlie Palmer belonged to the men's section, Surrey 19 and the women's was Surrey 38. Charlie trained at Edencroft in Station Road and used to go to Holbrook House in Shalford and be in a team on night duty ready to be called on if necessary.

Womens Voluntary Service

Many women who were at home worked for this organisation, mostly part time. It was the largest voluntary body of women workers in the country. In Bramley they helped with the evacuees, provided canteens for the troops, set up a second hand clothing shop and took part in the Rural Pies Scheme.

The Threat of Invasion

Joy Perun

The Smithbrook brickworks were closed during the war. My father who worked there before the war used to keep an eye on them. I remember that I once went with him to the brickworks. When he opened the door, inside were a number of little brightly coloured aeroplanes. My father said "Look in there girl....but keep your mouth shut." He later told me these were models that would be used as decoys in the event of invasion.

Joy gave the WWII Defence Medal (pictured opposite), which was awarded to her father A. J. Edwards of Smithbrook, to Bramley History Society.

The Home Guard had a special section who had secret instructions on how to act if we were invaded.

INVASION.

Instructions issued by your local Emergency Village Committee.

You will be warned by Radio, Military, Police or Wardens when hostilities are in the near vicinity, whether martial law has been proclaimed or not. Church bells are rung only when paratroops are landed. The village may be isolated and nobody allowed on the roads.

Stay put—which means remain in your village near your home unless you are required for a public duty.

FOOD. See separate pamphlet issued by Voluntary Food Officer.

EVACUATION. If for military reasons your house or street has to be cleared, you will be warned by the Military, Police or Wardens. Notice will be short, so have ready a **blanket, warm clothing, raincoat, gas-mask, ration book, identity card, any important papers, bottle of water, food in handy form**, and a spade. If you have a cycle and are not using it for essential work, immobilise it by hiding handlebars or pedals. You will then be conducted to a pre-arranged place.

WATER. Main water supply may fail, so fill buckets, bath, etc. When you know it has failed, you must conserve all your house water for drinking. W.C.'s must on no account be used—make a small latrine in your garden. Houses with wells which can supply their neighbours will display a notice "WELL WATER." In case of urgent necessity water may be fetched from depots at the Allweather Grouting Co. yard in Hall Road and Birtley Farm (Mr. Lyon). All water is drinkable after boiling or chlorination.

FIRE. Try to put it out yourself with neighbourly help. Do not depend on fire services as they may be engaged elsewhere.

REFUGEES. You must be prepared to take in and help the homeless and wounded. Give washing facilities to those contaminated by liquid gas.

RUMOURS. These will be spread by Fifth Columnists. Believe nothing unless it come from someone of whom you are sure, or over the radio in a voice you recognise. Give no information to anyone you do not know. Remember, one who speaks English is not necessarily a patriotic Briton.

SUSPICION. Report any suspicious, defeatist talk or actions to the nearest soldier, policeman or warden.

NOTICES. The only official notice board is at the local Constable's house. Ignore all others.

GAS. Be prepared for gas. Have your respirator and some anti-gas ointment No. 2 handy.

SLIT TRENCHES Dig a trench in your garden, 5 or 6 feet deep by 1 foot 6 inches wide. Trenches should be in the shape of a + It is excellent protection against dive-bombing and aerial machine-gunning.

EMERGENCY HEADQUARTERS. This will be situated at Edencroft, Station Road.

REGISTRAR. Casualties should be reported as soon as possible to the Village Emergency Registrar—Mr. Grinstead—at Emergency Headquarters, giving such particulars as cause of wound or death, place, time, etc.

LABOUR CORPS. Volunteers for clearing work, etc., with pick and shovel, should report at once to Emergency Headquarters. For further particulars apply to Mr. Parsons (Senior), who is Emergency Labour Officer.

MESSENGERS. All strong boys and girls are urgently wanted as messengers. Apply now to Captain Edgar.

REST CENTRE. Village Hall for homeless and refugees.

MOTOR VEHICLES. If these are in danger of capture put them completely out of action. Tractors are especially useful to the enemy. Diesel-engined vehicles should have injection pump and connection removed. Empty all petrol.

Every able-bodied man or woman will be called on for work—e.g., digging trenches, burying dead, filling sandbags, communal cooking, etc. Give your names in now to Mr. Parsons, so that you can be organised.

Remember the Parish may be isolated and we shall have to do everything ourselves to keep things going

F. N. FARGUS,
On behalf of the Village Committee.

August 1942.

WORK

All adults were caught up in the war effort. In October 1939 men between the ages of 18 and 32 were conscripted, and gradually others up to 41 years were called up. In the spring of 1941 all women between the ages of 18 and 60 had to be registered, and those without dependents were directed to serve in the Forces or Reserved Occupations.

Many men, some unfit to fight, were directed to Reserved Occupations which were for munitions, farming, those in the food industry, medicine, communications, government and local administration. It was very much the norm then that women gave up outside jobs on marriage; indeed, the Civil Service and many other organisations insisted on it. By 1943 90% of single women and 80% of married women were employed either in full or part-time in the war effort.

Double summertime

Double summer time (2 hours in advance of GMT) was introduced and was used for the period when normally ordinary summer time would have been in force. During the winter clocks were kept one hour in advance of GMT. This meant that there was a saving of power. Farmers used tractor headlights when ploughing late into the dark evenings.

Robin Hill

Double summer time meant long summer evenings, one night getting a hiding for staying to watch the Canadian 48th Highland Band beat retreat close to Bramley School. The downside was the need for cycle lamps on the morning paper round.

Winter nights, by contrast, were gloriously starlit with the absence of street lighting in the blackout. Wearing metal heel protectors we could make satisfying showers of sparks by running down the road and scuffing the ground vigorously.

Beryl Freeman

We did not like double summertime at first. In winter we went to work in the dark and came home in the dark. However in summer it was light by 8am to go to work. It was lovely to have the light evenings. We could come from work at 8pm and we could still go out because it was light until nearly midnight.

Factory Work

Geoffrey Knapp and his sister Hazel Mulkeirins, Angela Harms, Bob Hamilton and Dorothy Lee all had fathers who worked at the Dennis Brothers' factory in Guildford. Gordon Hedger's father was away from home working in a munitions factory.

Marshall, Hardy & Headland - MHH

The MHH factory was bombed in Kennington and it moved to Tannery Lane, Bramley, which, though just outside of the parish, was a significant employer of villagers. The MHH day shift was 8am to 8pm, the night shift 8pm to 8am, and Saturdays from 8am to 1pm. The factory employed dozens of local people, pictured later in this chapter.

Beryl Freeman

Every woman without responsibilities had to register. I had my interview on Thursday and had to leave my previous job and start work at MHH the following Monday. I hated the work and was always covered in oil and never felt clean and always seemed to stink of oil. Like a lot of people at that time we had no bathroom and I had to get out the tin bath and boil the copper when I wanted a bath. I hated the work, but it was bearable as there was a wonderful spirit of comradeship at the factory. The factory made bolts from big bars of hardened steel and we "pipped" the head taking off the excess steel knob on the top with a revolving wheel.

Michael Grant

I remember that we used to find vinegar and pickles in the machinery at the MHH, Hayward's pickle factory had been next door and had also got bombed! The first part of the factory was set up in the old part of the tanyard. The floors were still thick with chemicals used for tanning. The men in the 'auto' shop used to wear wooden clogs because of the oil and chemicals underfoot. If you wore soft rubber shoes the soles would soften and spread and become unwearable. They made undercarriage switch indicators and identification lamps and aircraft hardware.

Jimmy "Dixie" Dean was the foreman who had come with the firm from London. Every afternoon during the war, elderly, sometimes rather gentrified ladies would come in for a couple of hours to work on a voluntary basis.

Doreen Sykes

I volunteered to work at the MHH and was told to start the next day. At first the factory had no glass in the windows and we worked wearing our overcoats to keep warm. The factory made small parts for the dashboards of aircraft and tank bolts. We worked with capstans, lathes and electric drills. Each weekend four of us would do fire watching. The workforce who came with the factory was billeted in the village. I stayed working there until 1945. I enjoyed my time there, we all helped each other out and stayed late if necessary to finish things. We used to be provided with sandwiches at lunchtime, which was appreciated at times when food was rationed.

Georgina Harvey

My widow's pension was only ten shillings a week. So I applied for a job at the MHH. I worked in the inspection department and earned 10d (4p) an hour, I worked very long hours and had very little life besides work.

Other Factories

Avis Day, nee Turmaine

Betty Parsons and I worked at the James Walker's Works at Mill Lane Godalming. Inside the factory gates were wooden steps leading to a small machine shop where the men worked. The factory consisted of two floors; I worked on the lower floor making various gaskets. The material was hard asbestos, some by the name of graphite; I also worked with copper. I used a hammer and chisel on the thick asbestos, the thin I cut with shears. There were different size punches for the holes also hammered out by hand.

Avis Day still has her works pass

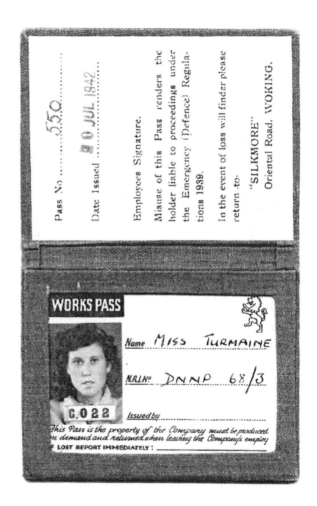

Arthur Dunn

I worked at Vulcanised Fibre Ltd, Broadford, Shalford, helping make fibre petrol tanks for the aeroplanes. These were attached to the outside of the plane and could be jettisoned to make craft lighter and faster coming home. So I was in a Reserved Occupation until 1943, then I applied to join the Home Guard but was called up and joined the Coldstream Guards at Pirbright.

Gladys Lucas

I was a trained hairdresser but needed to go into a reserved occupation to avoid being directed away from home. There was a clerical vacancy at Vulcanised Fibre Ltd, Broadford Mill, Shalford. I applied and got it. I worked in the cutting shop, where I had a little cubbyhole where I prepared the worksheets for the day's orders, and helped with handling the sheets of vulcanised fibre later in the day. Their edges were sharp, you could get cut easily.

I had a wonderful time there. Everyone was so friendly, there were always jokes with the drivers coming in to collect deliveries. My hairdressing came in useful too, I used to cut people's hair in the dinner hour.

Administration & Services

Cecily Taylor

I married in April 1940. It was the rule of those days that married women had to leave the Civil Service. My husband was away at war, and I was living at home with my parents. I got a job at Troughton and Young, electrical engineers, based at Birtley House, who were evacuated with all their staff from London. They organised work on electrical equipment for airfields. I was a shorthand typist, but I didn't use much of my shorthand, I mostly checked time sheets and the number of men working on airfields.

Joan Goodwin

People were needed to do war work and I could drive. I wished to continue living at home to be with my mother. I heard there were vacancies for drivers with Surrey County Council Highways Department. I was employed as a driver and was based at the Bramley Depot. I drove lorries full of tarmac or concrete to build Alfold by-pass and then Dunsfold Aerodrome. Another of my duties was very unpleasant, it was emptying soil buckets from the outside lavatories. I would start at 4am at the far end of Eastwood Road, Bramley. We used to call the collection lorries the 'violet carts'. I also had to clear road drains for which I had a long scoop, and I used to drive the lorry with the snowplough.

Christine Waller

My father worked as a driver at Bottings Mill, Chilworth. He used to deliver flour all round the area, but also went up to the London Docks to collect cereal. I fussed to go with him and, although my mother was very against it, I took a day off school and went with him. I enjoyed the ride but was disappointed. Because of wartime security, I wasn't allowed to go right into the Docks, but had to stay in the guardhouse. Then I was very worried that my Dad wouldn't come back for me!

Betty Brockman.

I left school at 14 in 1943 and went to the Guildford Post Office. At first I worked in the Telegraph Room, then spent time in the Telephone Room. I cleaned the switchboards and collected the tickets, the Guildford Exchange was manual, so details of every call had to be written out by hand. The Exchange was in Leapale Road and when the sirens went we would go up a lane to Bell House, the new building, and go down in the basement where there was an emergency switchboard.

Agriculture and Horticulture

As well as the Land Girls, 75,000 Italian Prisoners of War who were living in England in 1943 were allowed under escort to work on farms.

Fred Waller

I often went and helped on the Rydinghurst farm and was taught to drive there when I was 11. The 'War Ag', War Agriculture Committee, had a depot at Gaston Gate. Tractors were sent out to farms to help with ploughing. They came to Brooklands as there were only horses there.

The Land Girls were usually sent out from their billets to farms where they were needed, sometimes they were in huts, but at Sachel Court, Alfold, they lived in the house. I left school before the end of the war and went to work at The Hallams Farm for the Croombs. Although the family had moved to Shamley Green, they still rented the Rydinghurst land and I ploughed up 80/100 acres of pasture that had never been ploughed before. The job of ploughing, cultivating and seeding took weeks.

Dick Turrell

I attended Bramley School. I was told it was no good me staying there.

The Labour Exchange sent me to work for Fred Covey at Hurst Hill Farm. He used to ring up Surrey War Agriculture every Saturday and say how many men he wanted working on the farm the following week. Each day a coach would bring some prisoners of war, either Italian or German, and take them away again at the end of the day. They were good workers. They did not get paid, but the lady on the farm had to give them a meal. I worked there for the rest of the war and never had a day off. We used to drive the sheep from Hurst Hill along Bramley High Street to Bramley Golf Course. There were three dogs, a shepherd, a Land Army girl and myself. We used to cut the hay at the Grange Field belonging to the Bramley Grange Hotel. We used to get lovely hay from there.

The late David Elliott

Extract from '50 Not Out'

A History of Cranleigh & South Eastern Agricultural Society.
I well remember coming home on leave from Normandy and finding my father had six German prisoners of war living in our granary. It seemed very odd to me at the time, but I soon understood that necessity breeds strange bed fellows. One prisoner of war actually gave me a wooden pipe, carved from the wood of one of our pear trees, in recognition of my father's kindness to them.

Adrian Elliott, son of David Elliott and present owner of Whipley Manor Farm

At Whipley Manor Farm, the south side of Run Common between the old railway bridge and the canal had its common land status lifted during the war, and this was never re-instated afterwards. It was ploughed and a crop of potatoes planted, but flooding meant it was never harvested and the area was put back to grass.

Gladys Gill

I worked at Rushett Farm house, inside, but as the war took all the farm workers Mr Lyon asked me if he could get me to work on the farm. Would I do that, so I said yes. So he did get letters to say I would be a Land Girl. He had the papers to say so. So I started at 6.30 am and did housework up to ten o'clock. Then I was out on the farm for the rest of the day, doing haymaking and harvest, getting the cows in for milking, hedge cutting, hoeing in the fields, looking for eggs as the hens were free-range, picking up potatoes when they was being lifted and digging the vegetable garden.

When the nights got dark I was back in the house and left at 6.30 pm to bike home to Smithbrook.

The late David Elliott

During the war Father was on the War Agriculture Committee. Every field and meadow was analysed and the farmer was told to plough it. There was only Thorpe's Orchard in this area where the soil was considered not good enough to be worth the labour of ploughing, so they left it to grass. All the fields on the way to Horsham used to be white with cowslips, but they were all ploughed up.

Evelyn Nash

Fuel was quickly rationed. Out from the large greenhouse at Gosden Nursery went the pots of flowering plants for Christmas and in came lettuces, which needed minimal frost protection. In summer it yielded a heavy crop of tomatoes. Many more vegetables were grown, and I remember having to help pick peas and three sorts of beans for the market. The main worry was labour. From a staff of seven, gradually the men went to war or into munitions work. My father had been gassed in WWI and suffered frequent bad health and at one point the only able-bodied worker was a Conscientious Objector. My mother did a lot of the spring bedding plant pricking out, helped by my sister after her factory work and me after school.

EVERYDAY LIFE

Adults, whether in reserved occupations such as office, factory or agricultural work, or harassed housewives, had precious little leisure time in the war. People were coping with a day job that was five and half or six days long, doing voluntary work in the evenings and often night duties as well.

Housewives, as well as juggling housework, cooking and childcare, were spending long hours queuing for the scarce unrationed foods. It was a joke that if you saw a queue, you joined it, just in case.

Transport

Beryl Freeman

I can remember my mother getting up early to catch the bus to go and queue up for cakes and fish in Guildford High Street.

David Hooper

The buses that served the village were Hammonds' Bus Service, and the Aldershot and District Traction Company. There must have been about 5 or 6 buses an hour, from 6.30 am to 10 pm. They were well used and most had people standing. Sometimes you couldn't get on and had to wait in a queue for the next one.

Avis Day

Betty Parsons and I worked at the James Walker's factory at Mill Lane Godalming. We had to leave home by 7.30 am. As usual we took the shortest route on our cycles across Gosden Common and then through the sewage farm over the stile, picking up your cycle, wrapping it round your waist, step on stile, step over, step down. Fine in summer months, very tricky on dark mornings and evenings as dynamo lights went completely out on stopping.

Lilian Hampshire

I would walk down to Bramley from Thorncombe Street, usually pushing the pram. My wife's allowance for my husband's Army pay came as a pay slip. I had to take it to Bramley Post Office to cash.

Leisure

The main source of entertainment for most was the radio, for war news, general information and light entertainment. Tommy Handley's half hour comedy programme ITMA on the BBC did wonders for national morale and is fondly remembered by many. Newspapers, with newsprint severely limited, had little space for anything other than daily news.

Surrey Advertiser,
25th November 1939

To obtain funds for the purchase of dartboards for the troops, a largely attended dance was held at Bramley Village Hall on Wednesday. Mr Eric Shonfield was the chief organiser, and Eric Withyman supplied the music. The dance resulted in a profit of £9.7s 6d, (£9.37p) which will purchase 25 dartboards.

The Village Hall became a servicemen's canteen, a NAAFI, run by the YMCA and WVS, so communal meeting places were limited to the 'little hall' (a corrugated iron hut next to the village hall) and the upper room at St Faith's in Station Road. Occasionally events were permitted at St. Catherine's School and Bramley Grange Hotel.

Dick Turrell

The extra people living in the village brought trade to the village shops. Pubs could not get hold of beer so they closed. However Mr Gill at The Wheatsheaf had another pub in Kingston and got enough beer for himself and Les Warn at the Jolly Farmer so that all during the war they were able to open as usual.

Bernard Hill

As part of the programme to keep the public informed on activities of the Royal Air Force, an information unit would visit Bramley Grange Hotel on a Sunday afternoon and set up a cinema in the lounge. The films were of a pilot's view of aerial dogfights and the destruction of enemy aircraft. Very exciting for us youngsters and excellent as morale boosters.

Only the occasional dance appears to have been held at St. Catherine's School. Girls had to travel to Guildford or other villages for entertainment.

Doreen Sykes

I remember we used to go to the pictures in Guildford. When the sirens went we all had to come out and I remember walking home to Bramley. We used to 'walk one' and 'run one' from lamppost to lamppost. The last bus always left before the end of the film.

Betty Browne

My friend Joan and I used to go to dances in other villages, including Hascombe, Milford, Godalming and Cranleigh, either in an army van or on bicycles. As both Army and Air Force were stationed in the area there was great competition for the girls' attention. I remember lots of fun and laughter. People made the best of a bad situation. Canadians provided the bands and the food. At dances at Park Hatch, Hascombe we got friendly with a group of Canadians who used to come to Sunday tea.

Proceeds will be handed to the Local Committee of

WARSHIP WEEK

THE LOCAL HOME GUARD

Announce that a

DANCE

will be held (by kind permission of the Headmistress) in

The Speech Hall
St. Catherine's School
BR · · L · Y
on

MONDAY, APRIL 6th, 1942

Dancing 8 p.m. — 12 Midnight.

R.A.F. DANCE BAND

(FARNBOROUGH) will be in attendance.

SPOT & NOVELTY PRIZES

Evening Dress Optional.   Light Shoes Must be Worn

Tickets: 5/- Double   3/- Single

May be obtained from the Officers, N.C.O.s and members of the Local Platoon Home Guard.   NOTE the sale of Tickets is Strictly Limited.
Right of Admission Reserved.

A. LONGHURST, Printer

Fund Raising Weeks

Many of the social events were inevitably linked with fund raising for what was termed The War Effort. Various official Weeks, Salute the Soldier, Warship, War Weapons, Wings for Victory, etc., saw the school children designing posters and giving gym displays. The voluntary services organised parades, street collections and local societies ran whist drives.

Of the various Weeks, the Wings for Victory Week seems to have been especially busy and successful.

The sky's the limit in our—

WINGS FOR VICTORY WEEK

Grand scrappers—those lads up there. Show 'em we're fighters too . . . show 'em how we fight with them—with our work and our savings to help give them all the aircraft they need. Save more and help to straddle the target figure set for this district in "Wings for Victory" Week. Deny yourselves to save—help our district win its "Victory Wings"—with more and even more savings.

PUT EVERYTHING INTO IT—

3% Savings Bonds 1960-70
2½% National War Bonds 1951-3
3% Defence Bonds
Savings Certificates
Savings Stamps
Post Office Savings Bank
Trustee Savings Bank

May 15th - 22nd

HAMBLEDON R.D.

TARGET £250,000

The cost of 25 assorted aircraft

Surrey Advertiser

22nd & 29th May 1943
Hambledon Rural District decided to have its "Wings for Victory Week" May 15th to May 22nd 1943. They had a target to raise £250,000 (the cost of 25 assorted aircraft) Bramley, Blackheath and Wonersh set out to get £37,000. Bramley's target was £24,000, but made £60,000. The total made by the three villages was £83,253. Total by Hambledon Rural District: £634,737.

Four distinguished airmen spoke at the inaugural meeting at St Catherine's School. Following that there was a fun fair, white elephant stall, exhibition of munitions made from salvage, then a gymnastic display from the girls at St Catherine's. A dance was held at the Bramley Grange Hotel. There was a big church parade on Sunday. RAF films were shown, Snowdenham House was opened to the public, a fancy dress football match was held at Gosden Common and children's sports at Gosden House.

Individuals donated money; somebody donated £23,000. Selling centres and street group savers also played their part. The Home Guard gave a demonstration at Barnett Hill field, a bridge tournament was held at the Bramley Grange, and the Bramley Women's Fellowship organised a whist drive at St Faith's.

Other Group Activities

Surrey Advertiser
19th September 1942

Cricket matches between teams from the Jolly Farmer Hotel and the MHH Engineering Company on Gosden Common raised £4.12s 9d for the Red Cross. In the first game the company won by 4 runs (54-50) and on the second on Sunday the Jolly Farmer side were victorious by one (44-43).

The Bramley Women's Fellowship

The Women's Fellowship had been founded in 1920. Before the war they ran a lively programme of talks, whist drives, dances, and parties, but wartime restrictions curtailed many of these. However, the whist drives and fund raising for the war effort continued, and a full account of all money raised still exists (shown opposite). They met at St. Faith's in Station Road.

Surrey Advertiser
7th November 1942

Organised by Jean Verstage and Ivy Whiting aged 12 and 13, a sale of jumble and other articles was held at Oakdene, Birtley Road, Bramley on Saturday. Competition winners were E. Liddicott (beans in bottle) and R. Cheesemore (lucky ticket).

Ivy Durrant, nee Whiting

I don't remember what this was in aid of. I think Auntie Nellie, Jean's mother, did most of the work!

The late Pat Jackson and Ralph Durrant

In 1939, when the war brought evacuees, membership of the choir increased and girls were admitted. The church in wartime was often packed for Matins, in addition to the usual village congregation there would be soldiers from Snowdenham Hall, Bramley Park, and Chinthurst Hill and contingents from the Auxiliary Fire Service, The Home Guard, the Air Raid Precautions, the Red Cross and the Scouts. Occasionally there was a military band from Stoughton Barracks.

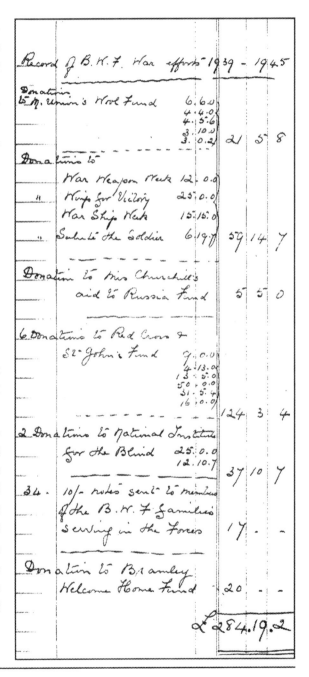

News From Home

Avis Day

Most evenings were spent writing endless letters. To my brother Raymond of the Grenadier Guards serving in the Middle East with the 8th Army and then the landing at Salerno, Italy. Letters to my stepfather James Penny, Royal Corp Signals also Middle East, then Sicily and Italy. Also letters to many of the lads we knew. I wanted desperately to go in the Forces but felt duty bound to look after my mother and sister Maureen.

Surrey Advertiser
Christmas Post
27th December 1941

With an ever-increasing population the post at Bramley Post Office has been a record. It was the busiest ever with both parcels and packets. Greetings cards especially for those serving abroad were very numerous. Extra staff and transport was obtained and thanks to the admirable organisation by Mr A.S.Noble the sub postmaster everything was cleared for Christmas Day.

Savings

The National Savings Scheme was started in 1939. People were encouraged to buy savings certificates or stamps. The Red Cross set up another scheme 'The Rural Pennies Fund' where weekly door to door collections were made.

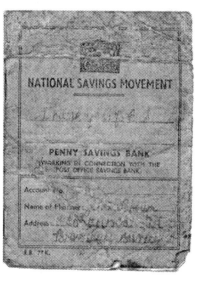

Ula Oakley

Mr Blunden organised the collection of War Savings. I was only about ten years old and I used to collect the stamps every Saturday morning and then went up Eastwood road selling them. I would then take the money back to him.

John Brown

I took my National Savings Book to school every week, and the teacher entered in my contribution. I still have the book and have never cashed the savings.

Church Bells - 1942

After the victory of El Alamein in late 1942 the Government decided the restriction on bell ringing should be suspended between 9 am and noon on Sunday 15th November.

Surrey Advertiser
Bramley
21st November 1942

The Parish Church bells were rung on Sunday from 10.45 to 11.15 am, and members of the Civil Defences services attended the morning service. The Rev. G.N Selby-Lowndes officiated.

Recycling & Salvage

National Salvage Drive - July 1940

This great drive encouraged the nation to collect anything that could help the war effort. Everyone was asked to hand over aluminium utensils, and all types of scrap metal from razor blades to garden railings. There was a shortage of paper due to the Atlantic Blockade, and of timber from northern Europe. Paper was needed for ration books, identity cards, and posters. Old woollen clothes were unpicked and volunteer knitting circles made socks and jerseys for the troops. Old sheets were made into bandages. Kitchen waste was collected to feed pigs, goats and chickens. In Hall Road a large storage building was taken over for bailing waste paper and sorting scrap metal.

Michael Grant

Like other boys I had a box on wheels. It had a brake and I could sit in it and travel around. I used to start at Links Road and then go to Gosden Common to collect newspapers. I took the clean ones to the butcher's and the rest to an old derelict shop opposite the butcher's that used to be Johnny Booker's Antique shop. The ladies of the WVS to whom I gave them, would give me chocolate in return. There was a request for horse chestnuts. I collected a huge amount from Gosden Common and the Bramley Grange Hotel.

The local milkman employed by Lymposs and Smee helped me take them to the Guildford Civic Hall. We were given thirty shillings (£1.50) for them.

Excerpts from 'The Smallholding'

2004

Basil Blythman

The war was good to my father. He won a contract with the Ministry of Supply on the 21st February 1940, my fifth Birthday, to collect waste paper in quantities in excess of 10 cwts from every parish in Hambledon Rural District to buy for resale. He collected bales of paper on three days each week and transported complete loads at least twice a week, always Saturdays to a paper mill in Summerstown, South London, and with deliveries for Southern Railways and re-cycling of glass, metal, and rags, money was not tight. The smallholding received subsidies on cattle feed; petrol coupons for the lorry and van; and it also provided milk, chickens, and pork. This linked to visits to Canadian Army camps at Unstead Park, Snowdenham Hall, and Bramley Park to collect pig swill. The Army provided most other things subject to War Time rationing.

Parish Magazine
February 1944

A Book Drive has been organised by the W.V.S. for the benefit of the forces to take place at Bramley from 12th-26th February. Residents are asked for their co-operation in this effort by turning out all their books they no longer require and which they consider would be suitable for general reading. The books will be collected by children from the schools and taken to the central depot at Forrest Stores. The target for Bramley is 5,000.

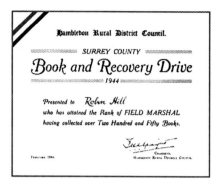

Robin Hill was proud to achieve Field Marshall rank at the tender age of 11

Comforts for the troops
Ena Baldock, Lord Wandsworth College, Gosden Common

When I was at the boarding school we were encouraged to knit socks and balaclavas for soldiers and airmen, we used to put little notes in them but I expect they were taken out before they were sent.

Parish Magazine
November 1943

The Bramley working parties organised by Mrs E. Kilburn have certainly not been idle since their inception in October 1939. They have made the following garments:- Forty shirts, twenty four vests, eleven pants, fifty four bags, also knitted garments included two hundred and sixteen scarves, two hundred and eighty eight pairs of socks, eighty two pullovers, forty one pairs of sea boot stockings, seventy nine pairs of gloves and twenty two caps. These have all been dispatched to the services and prisoners of war through the Guildford depot. Excellent work, reflecting great credit to all concerned.

The Convalescent Home
Doreen Sykes

Bramley Manor became a convalescent home for wounded soldiers. I used to see the boys walking around the village in their blue uniforms with red ties.

John Brown

I played with the Bramley Children's Orchestra in the grounds of the Convalescent Home at Bramley Manor to entertain the men. The 'Daily Mirror' took a photograph of us there. I also remember the Red Cross painted on the gatepost and the blue uniforms the men wore.

Surrey Advertiser
19th February 1943

A party was held by the British Red Cross Society detachments Surrey 38 (women) and Surrey 19 (men) at the Jolly Farmer, Bramley on Wednesday last week. About fifty six members of the detachments were able to attend. Several friends were invited. Dr Paterson cut the cake, which was presented by the matron and staff of Bramley Convalescent Home and made from their own rations in recognition of work done at the home by the detached members. Refreshments were supplied by Mrs Warn of the Jolly Farmer and were greatly appreciated.

Junior Activities

Red Cross Cadets

A Cadet unit was formed in Bramley in April 1943 by Commandant Mrs Roupel. Ann Bradley, Betty Brockman, Freda Carpenter, Gordon Hedger, Patricia Blythman, Robin Hill and many others attended classes in First Aid at Edencroft House. Geoffrey Hill is pictured on the right opposite with another cadet at Albury Park.

Mrs Brown's Gym and Dancing Club.

Betty Brockman

I was in Mrs Brown's gym and dancing club. We used the gym at St. Catherine's School. I remember the vaulting horse and the wall bars; it was a Nissen hut type of building. We put on displays.

Ula Oakley

I was at Bramley School until 1942. Mrs Brown used to teach dancing. I was partnered with Jane, her daughter. One Saturday morning we danced for the troops at the Odeon in Guildford.

Nancy Smith

My group danced the Teddy Bears' Picnic at the Odeon. Unfortunately my costume was too tight (I was a bit plump) and it split at the back, so I was instructed to dance facing the audience while the rest of them went round me

The 1st Wonersh and Bramley Scout and Wolf Cubs.

The boys helped in various ways. The picture shows the Wolf Cubs, mostly Bramley boys, on their Saturday morning salvage collection. They also collected cardboard and jam jars.

Bramley Juvenile Orchestra

The Bramley Children's Orchestra is well remembered. Hazel Mulkeirins didn't really want to join, but her mother insisted! Barbara Gall's mother helped organise functions and kept the books.

How many can you identify? The names of the band members are printed on page 47.

Ann Bradley

Captain Edgar had a pet monkey which had clothes on, was on a lead and used to sit on his shoulder when he visited us in the tin church hall.

Margaret Macnamara

In 1947 Captain Adgey-Edgar who was our patron bought two German prisoners of war to hear us play. The prisoners of war were stationed at Stoughton. They then played for us. I got the prisoners of war to sign my autograph book, the date 6th August 1947. On 12th September we gave a concert in the village hall. The Juvenile Band playing one half and the German soldiers band playing the other.

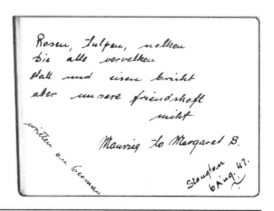

Bob Harris's account sums it all up

Bramley Juvenile Band was formed in 1944 following a suggestion in the *Parish Magazine* by Capt. W.H.Edgar who later became the Orchestra's Hon organiser. His idea was met with immediate enthusiasm and with Mr A. H. Lane from Woking as teacher/conductor, the children aged between 8 and 14 years old practiced for two hours each week in the small Church Hall.

Mr Lane, aged 72, cycled from Woking. The practice night consisted of one hour split into instrument groups for individual instruction and then the whole orchestra played together.

In early 1945, after 4 months, the orchestra consisting of 20 members played its first concert at St. Catherine's School hall. Shortage of instruments prevented many eager young musicians from joining, however attics and second hand shops were scoured, and Mr Lane spent many hours repairing badly damaged instruments.

By March 1945 the orchestra of nearly 50 members was playing regularly at local fetes, concerts, W I meetings and garden parties. The programme of about 12 numbers, some including solo parts, were folk melodies or composed by Mr Lane to avoid copyright fees.

The cost to the children was 3 shillings (15p) a month, those who found it difficult to afford instruments were financed by Capt. Edgar and repaid the money to him over a period.

The usual orchestral fee for a performance would be to supply a coach, pay Mr Lane travel expenses and provide refreshments for the orchestra. The children rated the organisers by the quality of their food!

The children played together for about five years, but as they grew up they found other interests and in the early 1950's the orchestra faded out of existence.

The Turning Tide

In September 1944 the Dim Out was introduced.

Blackout precautions had to be observed only if the siren sounded, and in April 1945 full street lighting was permitted.

Everyday life was easier, and a church youth club had begun. Among the leaders were Mary Templeman and Russell Wadsworth from the school and the curate, Mr. Harris. There were social activities in St. Faith's and the Little Hall. Ballroom dancing classes were started in St. Catherine's Speech Hall.

Christine Waller

The ballroom dancing classes at the Youth Club were very popular. But one evening Miss Kilburn, who had been trying to get us to dance body to body, made us put sheets of newspaper between partners, and dance without holding each other. We didn't like it, we were all too embarrassed and she didn't do it again.

Nancy Smith

Two one-act plays were produced. We performed them in St. Catherine's Hall. I was Grandma in 'Mr Fothergill Joins the Angels'. Because I was sitting knitting all through the play, I had the prompt book on my lap. My long hair was powdered and done in a bun and my mother gasped when the curtain went up, as I looked exactly like my grandmother.

Surrey Advertiser
Home Guard entertains Children
6th January 1945

Bramley Home Guard helped by subscriptions by people in the district gave a party for over 250 children of school age in St Catherine's Hall on Saturday afternoon. The children obviously enjoyed a concert in which the band of the Bramley Children's Musical Society made their first appearance. Others taking part were Al Bones (comedian), 'Clown' Moore and the Bramley Gymnastic Club trained by Miss V. Morris. Each child received a bar of chocolate the coupons for which were given by the Home Guard and a 2 shilling (10p) savings stamp. The hall was lent by the Head Mistress, Miss Symes.

The Orchestra Members

			Captain Edgar	Mick Coleman	Mr Lane	Roy Fitt		
Ken Pearce	Mick Lewis	Dennis Hedger	Ralph Durrant	Duncan McKenzie	Robin Harris	Philip Baker	Keith Bothamley	

Ken Batchelor	Jean Verstage	Malcolm Watson	Hazel Rose	Iris Batchelor	Margaret Blythman	Dave Bentley	?	John Brown	Terence Gould	Jennifer Young
Tony Cramp	Jim Longhurst	Roy Turrel	Jim Baker	Roy Holder	Pat O'Hara	Angela Booker	Pat Stevens	Hazel Knapp	Brian Parsons	Basil Blythman
Basil Whitney	Audrey Longhurst	Barbara Gall	Anne Harris	Pauline Templeman	Mollie Gall	Gwen Jelley	Ray Redman	Keith Jelley	Tony Skilton	

SCHOOLS

Memories are strong about school life, with access to the Log Book, and inevitably we have most from Bramley Church of England School. Other schools at that time were the Lord Wandsworth College at Gosden House, St Catherine's and St Martha's both in Station Road and Grafham Church of England School.

The Lord Wandsworth College

Gosden House was the girl's branch of the College, it opened in 1919 and closed as an economic necessity in 1946. Gosden housed between 50 and 100 girls, at any one time, during its existence. These girls were considered orphans through the loss of one or both parents. Half the girls went to Guildford High School and the rest went to Godalming County Grammar School. In the earlier days younger children went to a local school. Gosden House and grounds provided work for a number of villagers both in the laundry and extensive grounds where most of the food to feed the girls was grown. It also boosted the numbers at Bramley Church on Sundays and considered itself part of the village.

Dorothy Booth

There was talk of evacuating the school to Scotland when war was imminent, but I suppose the logistics were very complicated. Air raid shelters were built and much used during the bombing of London. We put on siren suits and scooted over the lawn where we tried to sleep on bunks until the 'all clear', and dear old Mary Gainham kept us going with radio and music etc. I can remember the red glare in the skies over London when we re-emerged and at one point there were searchlights more or less opposite Gosden.

Ena Baldock

On Friday nights Matron had a shoe inspection. If they were not shining bright we lost our pocket money. One Friday just before shoe inspection the barn opposite the house went up in flames. As it was pitch darkness it would have been a beacon for enemy bombers overhead, so we quickly formed a chain and passed buckets of water to the men trying to put the fire out, it seemed an age until the fire brigade came. Needless to say I lost my pocket money because my shoes were wet and I felt quite aggrieved after my hard work. I cannot speak for the other girls. Matron was well aware what we had been doing, but praise was short in that area.

Grafham C of E School

Fred Waller

We had three teachers, Miss Bonney, Miss Power and Miss O'Kane, who all lived in the schoolhouse together. There were never more than about 70 to 80 children in the school, but they came from all over, Rushett and Run Commons, Goose Green, Elmbridge and Smithbrook. The children from Painshill caught the old 49 Alfold bus to school. All the children, including us, took packed dinners to school. When the war came, I had to help put the protection on the school windows. This was glued muslin, which you put into water and then stuck on the glass to keep the glass from flying off in splinters in the event of an air raid. I think I got the job as I was the only one who would go up the ladder!

We had some evacuees join our classes. Their teacher, a man, came too and was quite a shock after our three gentle lady teachers. I remember he had a very hard hand and often took us by the ear. Still, he took us out sketching with charcoal, something we'd never done before and we enjoyed looking at things through his microscope. He generally widened our experiences, so we forgave him his hard hand. The evacuees were just absorbed into the school, so we had full time teaching. We had no air raid shelters, if things got near we just went under the desks.

Bramley C of E School

1939

Log Book: 7th September

Mr Grimmett met the Headteacher of the London children and myself with a view to re-opening the school on 11th and arrangements were made accordingly. It was decided that Bramley children should take the morning session and the London children the afternoon session. I was to provide all stock and materials necessary for both sessions. Mr Blogg has been called to the Forces and is being replaced.

Log Book: 11th September

School re-opened in the morning at 8.45 am. 33 new entrants were admitted. Children were arranged in their new classes (now 5 instead of 4).

Full time education for the older children was established in October, when they used the Little Hall, which stood next to Village Hall.

1940

The cold winter was grim. The outside toilets across the playgrounds froze.

Log Book: 29th February

Coal supplies ran completely out and I had to resort to delivery myself from the coal yard with my car and transport sufficient for lighting up next day.

School shelters

These were constructed in the school garden using voluntary labour. The corrugated fence between the playground and cemetery was taken down and used to reinforce the trench. When the fence was taken down, the children were forbidden to go into the cemetery. They did, of course.

Michael Grant

You could tell the school shelters were built by World War I veterans - they were dug out properly, and had a buttress at the entrance against blast.

Robin Hill

The shelter was not big enough for we juniors. Air raids were spent in the cloakroom, the high windows of which were criss-crossed with sticky tape. We each had to provide a cushion on which to sit on the tiled floor under the coat racks with our gas masks hanging above.

Nancy Smith

I set up a 'shop' in the cemetery, and got into trouble for attracting other children, it didn't seem fair – everybody was going in there.

Bernard Hill

We were given time off school to pick potatoes in the autumn. We used to go to Nurscombe Farm where Minnie, the horse pulled the spinner. This threw the potatoes out which we then picked up and put in bushel baskets. I remember being told 'Boy, you have two hands – pick up the potatoes with both of them!' To our dismay at the end of the season we failed to be paid. A march was organised to the owner's house where we made our case. Fortunately we eventually did get our money.

The Blitz

Log Book: 26th August

An air raid siren sounded at 2 am in the morning; the children look rather tired this morning.

Log book: 6th September

I again put on record that the close pro ximity of the school to the main road often renders oral lessons utterly useless and frequently during the last few weeks the teachers have been unable to cope with the noise of military convoys and tractors passing. This has been practically continuous for two months.

Log Book: 11th September

The air raid alarm went at 11 am and the alert lasted 25 minutes. For the last four nights the alert has lasted about eight hours and the All Clear has not gone until 4 am approx.

Maureen Mills

We were having our weekly cookery lesson when the siren sounded, so it was down tools, pick up our gas masks and walk in an orderly fashion to the shelter in the school gardens. When we got in there we couldn't hear any signs of aircraft or bombs, so we soon got bored with being cooped up in the semi dark. The shelter had been dug in a zigzag pattern (I understand because of the blast) so, still wearing our white aprons, we pretended to be ghosts and made noises and jumped out on anyone coming along the shelter and thought we were very frightening. Eventually the 'All Clear' went and we were able to go home. I am afraid I cannot remember what happened to the cooking.

1941

Another bad winter, with fuels shortages, and measles, German measles and mumps were prevalent during much of the year. Although the Log Book does not show it, ex-pupils agree that Mrs Brown was in reality Acting Head by this time.

Michael Grant

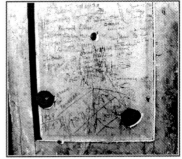

I used to carry the coal and milk crates to the classrooms. Once when I was in Mrs Brown's class her brother, Captain Harland, came to talk to us about the Merchant Navy Convoys. He was killed later. I went up in the tower and tied the bell up as none were allowed to be rung. Senior boys had the job of winding the clock in the tower. When the clock was restored in 1997, the board pictured opposite was discovered covered with the names of both village and evacuee boys, so many names that it is obvious that the tower was visited unofficially – possibly a 'dare'?

Betty Brockman

My father, Alfred Stevens, was school caretaker. He was officially due in school at 6.30, but often went early in the cold weather to get the fires going well. Later, when my mother took over the cleaning, the senior boys carried coal to the classrooms. She was paid 4s 0d (20p) a week to dust classrooms. In the holidays my parents and my sister Pat and I would go for the day. My father swept down the walls, scrubbed the desks and cleaned the windows. My mother scrubbed the floors. You could really the see the difference as she scrubbed away a term's dirt. I used to wash out the inkwells and clean the doll's house in Miss Smith's room.

My mother took over the job, with the help of Mrs Tanner of Brewery Cottages, by the Foundry, because my father was sent as Directed Labour to MHH. My mother and Mrs Tanner did the cleaning for a year and my father went back to the job after the war.

BRAMLEY C OF E SCHOOL (GYM CLASS)
EARLY 1940s
MISS B.STEVENS. MISS. C.LONGHURST MISS J.VERSTAGE
MISS. G WHITBOURN

1942

Log Book: 21st January

The School is carrying on under great difficulties. The lavatories are frozen, snow is very deep and we are one short of staff.

In March arrangements were made to amalgamate village and evacuee children for full-time schooling. Mr Brown was too ill to cope. After super-human work by Mrs Brown and the new caretaker, Mr Boxall, all through the Easter holiday classrooms were completely reorganised. There was also a complete absence of any coal coke or wood for heating.

The Staff: Mr Brown (headmaster), Mr Wadsworth (from London), Mrs Goodman (from Croydon), Mrs Brown, Mrs Templeman, Mrs Hilton and Miss Smith (Reception). There were 215 village children, 35 London and 16 Croydon, a total of 266. Classes were very full, especially in the upper school.

Evelyn Nash

Going back to school in April 1942 really stands out in my memory when we met Mr Wadsworth for the first time. We had seven evacuee children in our group and we all settled in well as far as I can remember. We loved Mr Wadsworth, he had a wonderful sense of humour, was always patient, but saw through any silliness right away. Suddenly, after so many changes, we had continuity and stability.

Robin Hill

Winters were cold, there was great competition in Mrs Goodman's class to sit close to the open fire and to claim a thawed bottle of milk at playtime. If we took an orange to school, Mrs Goodman would first remove the peel having scored it with scissors, claming it was to be candied rather than wasted.

On 24th May the Log Book notes the death of Mr Brown and on 27th May the School was closed for the afternoon session for his funeral service.

Log Book: 13th July

At a managers' meeting today Mr E. J. Chapple was appointed Head Teacher to take over duty on 4th August.

Log Book: 5th August

The Vicar, Chairman of the Managers, presented Mrs Brown, wife of the late Head Teacher, with a cheque for £8.5s. (£8.25) on the occasion of her leaving the district.

Christine Waller

We used to make posters for the various War Weeks. I won a prize for my 'Squanderbug' poster during the Squanderbug campaign. This was to persuade people to put their spare cash into War Saving and not just squander it.

Maurice Betts

When we made posters for the various 'Weeks', Ernest Mason, later of Bramley Players, used to come in and help with our designs and he also donated prizes.

Log Book: 18th November

The caretaker finished on Saturday. I have personally seen to the fires night and morning. The Vicar came in this morning to help me.

Surrey Advertiser
11th November 1942

The Bramley Church of England School children have during the past month collected one and a quarter cwt. (64kg) of horse chestnuts and one and a half cwt. (75kg) of rose hips. These have been distributed to manufacturers who need them for purposes connected with the national war effort. The money received has been put into the school fund.

1943

Log Book: 3rd September

The school attended church service this morning on the occasion of the National Day of Prayer.

Log Book: 26th November

School telephone number 2346 in operation.

1944

In mid-June the first of the V1s, the flying bombs, 'doodlebugs', appeared. There is no mention of doodlebugs in the Log Book.

Log Book: 16th October

As far as I can ascertain, the children who went potato picking during the holiday picked up some 200 tons (tonnes).

1945

Log Book: 8th May

Today and tomorrow being VE - Victory in Europe Day will be holidays.

20th October

Mr Blogg returned to duty after 6 years in the RAF

St Catherine's School

The school coped with the thirty evacuees from Brighton, air raids, the Home Guard in their grounds, shortage of domestic staff and still managed to continue with exams and house competitions in drama, music, public speaking and games. The annual garden party raised money for comforts for the Services and a full part was taken in the various Weeks and National Savings events. The staff helped at the local canteen and at weekends the senior girls helped at Barnett Hill and other hospitals. Finally, contributions were made to the Bramley Peace Commemoration Fund.

From a school magazine

Instead of fire drill we now have trench drill. We disappear in a long line hanging on to the person in front, and the mistress patrols up and down with a torch to see we are all present.

Apparently the younger children found it all exciting, not frightening and hoped there would be the chance to wrap up warmly over their siren suits and go out into the dark. Once in the shelters they talked and sang, though older people longed for a warm bed.

Later it was felt safer to used two-tier bunks in the Common Room on the ground floor, but parental worries about ventilation led to changes. The girls stayed in their dormitories until a warning sounded, then went down to the passages where the building structure was strongest.

With the arrival of the doodlebugs they learned to duck quickly under the desks as soon as they heard a buzz.

Elizabeth Rogers

I was a daygirl and cycled there each day. Miss Symes the headmistress was a distant benign figure who always wore her gown. Several of the staff were of pensionable age but they stayed on until the war was over.

Before the war we had maids who served our meals at the tables. Soon there were no maids and we cleared the tables ourselves. Our uniform was a pleated gymslip and Viyella blouses. Clothing coupons were short and the uniform rules were relaxed. We were constantly darning our lisle stockings.

I remember the display we did for the 'Wings for Victory Week'

The Rev Selby–Lowndes taught us cricket. He used to wear his cassock over his jodhpurs on his motorbike. These we called the 'vicar's knickers'. The Bramley Home Guard met at the Green Room at St Catherine's, after the war some Molotov cocktails were dug up in the shrubbery.

MISS AGATHA SYMES
Headmistress 1926 – 1947

Jean Hopwood

I cycled to school. I can remember how painful my hands were as they thawed after cycling to school in the cold weather. We all suffered from chilblains. The school was never very warm and we used to huddle round the luke-warm radiators. The food was the usual school food – I did not like bully beef or blackened potatoes!

We did lots of very spectacular gym displays with lots of marching and formation work. I vaguely remember the fund raising events at school. When I hear 'Colonel Bogey' played I am always reminded of the gym displays we did.

My mother bred cocker spaniels. One day I was called to the headmistress's study. I went there quaking. An ADC was there, who wanted a puppy for General Montgomery. He went to our address and chose one called Oliver. He was taken to France to the General. My sister Nancy later wrote to him to ask how Oliver was, and he wrote back a very nice letter saying that unfortunately he had been run over. General Montgomery renamed the puppy Rommel, after the German General.

The puppy is mentioned in letters and the General's biography.

St Martha's School

Sally Caton and Richard Christophers

The school owned and run by Miss Ball, occupied the two houses called Wood View and South View in Station Road. Fees were from £3 3s 0d (£3.15) a term. There were some boarders. The rooms were not huge, probably about 20 in each class. There was no space for sports, but drill was done, and also moving to music. Entertainments were put on. Richard recalled that a version of Snow White and the Seven Dwarfs was performed in the Wonersh Memorial Hall in aid of Barnardo's. There was no full uniform, the girls had Tana lawn pinafores and the boys a mauve tie.

MILITARY PRESENCE

Both the British and the Canadian armies were stationed at Bramley during the war. At Gosden Common and Rydinghurst there were permanent Searchlight Units run by the British Army. Snowdenham Hall, Unstead Park and Bramley Park were requisitioned by the Army and various British and Canadian regiments were stationed there. In 1942 the Canadian Army built Dunsfold Aerodrome.

Searchlight Units

Russell Hudson

The site of the searchlight on Gosden Common, was situated on the section of Common beside Foxburrow Hill Road, northwards to the boundary with the, now, police garage and workshops, flanking the main 281 Guildford to Horsham Road, and westwards to the rear entrance to the sewage farm, by Gosden Farm. The battery was maintained by a small company of approximately 15 men of the Royal Artillery, on a permanent, self–contained basis from 1940 to late 1943/4. The living quarters were situated to the rear of the site, the actual searchlight etc, was nearer to the main road. There was no permanent gun emplacement on the site, but it is recalled that on occasions a transportable Bofors anti aircraft gun was brought to the site and could be made quickly operational, although nobody can remember a shot being fired in anger. Apart from night times searchlight activities, it was understood to have been part of a line of repeater stations, relaying information to London of the number of enemy aircraft crossing our coastline en route for London and other cities during the Blitz.

Joan Grant

I was a papergirl at W. H. Smith's at Bramley and Wonersh Station when I was twelve or thirteen years old. I had a heavy red bicycle with a carbide lamp. My round started with Upper Links Road and Foxborough Road. Then I would enjoy the ride down the hill to where the searchlight was. The boys there would put me in front of the boiler and give me cocoa to warm me up.

Fred Waller

Rydinghurst House was requisitioned for Canadian troops, who parked their lorries under the trees along the farm drive so they were hidden from the air. There was also a Royal Artillery Searchlight unit on the farm, a dozen or more men in huts in the wood. I used to go down to visit them every evening and they taught me how to assemble and dismantle a Lewis gun. They didn't use the gun during the Blitz, but they did later on the doodlebugs and shot some down.

Snowdenham Hall

Bernard Hill

I was the paper boy who used to deliver the morning papers to the Canadian Sergeant's Mess which was in the grounds of Snowdenham Hall. The troops kindly saved covers from their Sweet Caporal cigarette packets for me. These had aircraft silhouettes printed on the back which were very collectible! The bases of the Nissen Huts are still visible today.

Bramley Park

Brian Harms

I remember a lot of different regiments were stationed at Bramley. The turnover at Bramley Park was such that sometimes as often as two weeks there was a soldier from a different regiment standing guard at the Park gates.

Bramley School Log book 15th May 1940

The unending stream of lorries and buses transporting soldiers made it almost impossible to continue work in school.

Nancy Smith

It must have been in Summer, 1940. I remember coming home from school and finding the lane full of army lorries and small tanks. I asked my mother 'Have we been invaded?' The soldiers, the Royal Artillery, went in the Park. Our cottage was the last, with a garden at front and side and there was only a narrow strip of wood, called the Shrubs by us, between it and the Park. I could look out of my bedroom window and see the bell tents. The soldiers were always in tents; there weren't any Nissen Huts. I used to talk to them, and gradually my mother put seats out in our garden and invited them round. She put up a dartboard in our outhouse, where the lav was, and they played there in the evenings. In winter evenings they came into our kitchen and played. Once their officer came round to make sure they were behaving well. He told my mother to make sure they left the garden tidy and the lav clean and thanked her for her kindness. At night there were always two soldiers on guard at the Park gates. My mother would send one of us down to tell them there was some cocoa made and they took it in turns to come up and have a welcome drink and warm up in the kitchen.

Ann Bradley

There were a lot of Canadians posted in the village. There was a sentry box at Home Park Gates. It was here that I first saw a coloured man. He told the children ghost stories and would scare them with large eyes rolling. The children were always treated well by the military during wartime and no harm came to any of them.

Dorothy Lee

The soldiers used to drive their jeeps down to Luxford's Garage in Birtley Road and fill the tanks up with petrol. They then used to give the children lifts back to Bramley Park and drop them off at the gates. I remember a convoy of soldiers driving through the village and the staff at Elwin's giving them fish paste sandwiches to eat.

People were asked to invite soldiers into their homes. The troops did exercises with the Home Guard, attended church parades, dances and of course the pubs!

Hazel Mulkeirins

My granny used to have a soldier, at least one, for tea, or just for a cup of tea or cocoa. You could not buy a thing. There was barely enough food to go round, so we did not have them coming to us. The soldiers used to walk round the villages in twos and threes and would give us children sticks of chewing gum from Canada. I wanted the war to go on for a long time so that I would be old enough to marry a Canadian soldier.

Mollie Hutton

My sister Barbara and I lived in Snowdenham Lane. We used to ask the passing soldiers for chewing gum, "Have you any gum chum?" Once the soldiers thought I was being a bit too cheeky and one of them picked me up and sat me on a high wall at the top of the lane and left me there. I could not get down. I cannot remember who rescued me, I think it was one of the neighbours.

Doreen Sykes

At times there used to be convoys of tanks that drove through the village. They made a lot of noise and I did not feel safe on the road on my bicycle so I used to ride on the pavement. Birtley Road snack bar was next to the Toll Cottage and the soldiers used to stop their lorries there, it was very popular.

Margaret Macnamara

During the war Canadian soldiers were stationed at Bramley Park. We used to see them in the village shops. They stood in the sentry boxes at the Park gates. This was the first time we had seen foreigners. We thought that their speech was very different from ours. There were some African Canadians. One Christmas our father went to the pub at lunchtime and began talking to a group of soldiers and asked them to come to our house for the afternoon. Later on five soldiers came. My dad got out the dartboard and taught them to play darts. They stayed for tea and went back to camp quite late. They came often on Sunday afternoons after that, always bringing sweets and chewing gum for us. They were involved later in the war in the Dieppe landings.

Two in particular stay in my mind, Joe Browne and Jack Fegan. After Dieppe, Jack Fegan came to see us and told us that Joe had been killed in action at Dieppe. Many years later my husband and myself visited Joe's grave. Jack Fegan wrote in my autograph book on 3rd October 1945 and put his service number D17078 after his name.

HERE'S To you as Good as you are HERE'S To ME as Bad as A am But as Good as you are and as Bad as A am S'm as good as you are as Bad as A om.

John Fegan. S.W.
D 17078.
R.CE.
Oct 3/45

Dick Turrell

We noticed a gradual build up of troops in the village long before D Day. In March 1944 the troops were marching on foot through Bramley and there were a lot of lorries parked along the roads. People brought tea and coffee out to them. The extra troops camped out under canvas in Bramley Park. I had previously seen them camping and with many tanks at Unstead Wood. After D Day, 6th June 1944, I cycled up there but they were all gone. The village and the surrounding area seemed suddenly to be empty and very quiet. When the peace came the soldiers left Bramley very soon and completely cleared up after them.

The XII Manitoba Dragoons

The Regiment, which was formed from other units, was stationed at Bramley from November 1942 until June 1943 and left for Tunbridge Wells in July 1943.

Gord Sim

Secretary XII Manitoba Dragoons & 26 Field Regiment Museum, Brandon, Manitoba, Canada

On November 1 1942 the 18th Car regiment under LT Colonel McMahon left Aldershot and was decentralized to the following estates and properties in Surrey,

Regimental Headquarters -- Snowdenham Hall	Headquarters Squadron ..... Northanger
A Squadron ------------------ Hallams at Blackheath	B Squadron .... Munstead Heath
C Squadron ------------------ Unsted Park	D Squadron .... Bramley Park

Gord Sim sent a short film with commentary, including shots of the Dragoons taking part in the Wings for Victory Week. It also shows a church service being taken in Bramley Park and their band leading the

Parade through the Park gates to the High Street. Behind them are various organisations including the Home Guard, Police, Fire Brigade, ARPs. Red Cross, Scouts and Guides.

John Grant

During one of the Weeks I remember the Home Guard, the Fire Brigade, Cadets etc. were in a parade. We were led from the Park by a band and the Manitoba Dragoons. There was a service in the Park that day, led by the Rev. Selby-Lowndes. Then we marched into the High Street. I'm not sure where we went.

This band is also recorded as playing at a dance in Shalford during Wings For Victory Week.

Surrey Advertiser

1st May 1943

The "Surrey Advertiser" has been asked by some of the lads of the "Canadian Army" to thank the people of Bramley and district for their hospitality, great welcome, and general kindness. Their experience they say has been a happy one. The writers wish their Surrey friends good health, good luck and a safe return of their lads after the Victory.

Herb Schuppert

Herb was stationed in Bramley with the Manitoba Dragoons during 1942-3 and sent this newspaper cutting about Caesar the dog from Bramley and found out that he was purchased for 'ten bob' (50p) just outside a pub at 11 o'clock by three troopers. He was taken back to Canada at the end of the war and died of old age aged fifteen.

Sergeant Everybody Loved

Caesar goes to his Blighty

Sgt. Caesar
... Joined Army as pup

Sergeant Caesar, formerly of 17th Troop of the 12th Manitoba Dragoons - probably the only sergeant in the Canadian Army who was loved by everybody - is dead.

Sergeant Caesar joined the Dragoons of the 18th Armoured Car regiment in 1942 at Bramley, England, when he was just a pup.

Of doubtful parentage, he soon proved that he had all the qualities of a thoroughbred and was adopted by the unit as its official mascot.

He obtained periodic promotions officially through regimental orders and eventually achieved the rank of sergeant. He served with the regiment throughout the war and was a favourite of all ranks despite the many problems he created in his various exploits.

At one time, while in France, "he was demoted" because he disappeared for a few days. "Must have been those French girls," one of his buddies observed. Later he was promoted again and given back his specially-made jacket with the three stripes on it.

"This is the longest fence I ever saw!"

Herb Schuppert also sent this cartoon from Army Daze, a booklet printed in Holland dedicated to the officers and men of the XII Manitoba Dragoons. The author Les Jordan was an American who joined the Dragoons in 1941 before the USA joined the war.

Coming home from the local Pub after closing we came upon a fellow as seen in the drawing from Les Jordan's Army Daze book. He told us that someone told him to follow the fence to the billet entrance gate and as he had more than his share of beer he just kept going around saying it was the longest fence he ever saw.

Dunsfold Aerodrome

The Canadian Army built Dunsfold Aerodrome in 20 weeks, it was fully operational by October 1942

Joy Perun

In 1942 Dunsfold Aerodrome was created. They moved the main road that ran through the middle and built the new road. It was my father's job to put lights across it when it got dark so that people did not go down it. I still call it the "New Road". Convoys of military vehicles drove by our house. We used to count the aeroplanes going out and coming back again; that is if and when they came back. So the skies were quite noisy then.

Joan Goodwin

I drove lorries full of tarmac or concrete to build Alfold by-pass and then Dunsfold Aerodrome with the Canadian soldiers. I used to tip out the tarmac from the lorry and then clear out what was left in the lorry with a big scraper. This used to burn holes in my shoes, which I was given extra clothing coupons for. There were no ladies toilets on site and if I made a visit a soldier would have to stand on guard outside! The Canadian soldiers were not exactly polite to me and called me 'A bloody Limey woman', but before long they realised I was a worker and a match to them.

Jim Chant

I was a fireman on the railway during the war and fired through Bramley. War goods did not come down this route as it was single track and the main line to Portsmouth was more convenient. But I do remember taking a few 28 truck trains to Dunsfold siding full of rubble from the Blitz in London. Canadian soldiers turned up in their trucks that they had previously travelled in to Dunsfold, to unload the rubble to build the bypass and the airfield.

Douglas Fisher, Manitoba Dragoons

It was from the hilltop on the way to Godalming, where one could briefly see the drome, that I saw my first Mustang fighter planes. They looked more like a Hurricane than a Spitfire but we'd heard naught about this aircraft until a pair of them went lancing over us by Northanger one morning. The proverbial English schoolboy know-it-all brought us up to snuff on the plane's identity.

The ones we saw had RAF markings and later this fitted with what we heard at Farnborough from plane buffs there that the Yanks had decided that the Mustangs, built for the Brits' needs, were better than anything they had. They took it up, accelerated production of these master fighters and about 13 months after seeing them over Northanger we were watching squadrons take off and head east a half hour or so after the B17 formations of 8th Air Force had gathered above Norfolk and the Wash, then straightened into tighter, path formation and went off, over the North Sea.

Lilian Hampshire

My sister Joyce Blythman met a Canadian soldier at a dance at St Catherine's School. She married him and went to Canada with a six month old child at the end of the war. He had a grandfather who was a full-blooded Indian. He was stationed at Dunsfold and the soldiers liked to come to the Jolly Farmer in Bramley. My mother used to have two or three soldiers to tea on Sundays. One young man wrote to his sister in Canada who sent her food parcels. He was later killed.

Joan Federchuk

In 1945 I married Peter Federchuk a Ukrainian Canadian. He was with the Canadian Army when they built Dunsfold Aerodrome. He was living at Park Hatch, Hascombe. He got demobbed here and worked on the farm milking cows and then he worked for Thomas's the builders. First we lived at my home and then we moved to Cranleigh. We went back to Canada to live in 1946.

Dunsfold was used to repatriate many thousands of prisoners of war between April and June 1945

Elizabeth Rogers

My mother was a VAD in the Red Cross. and wore an old fashioned uniform. She knew all the local evacuees. They often used to come to our house. She used to cycle from Wonersh to Dunsfold when they were re-patriating our soldiers who had been prisoners of war. On two occasions I borrowed her uniform and went to Dunsfold Aerodrome. When the planes landed the men jumped out. They were then deloused. The Red Cross worked in reception and generally looked after them and gave them a good meal before they were moved on. I remember the nightingales singing in the hedges.

Joy Perun

I remember my mother taking us children down to the "triangle" by Nanhurst to where the fountain is. Here we waved to lorry loads of prisoners-of-war having just been flown into Dunsfold Aerodrome. I remember one man dragging a flag with a swastika on it behind the lorry.

AERIAL ACTIVITY

The spring of 1940 was a dark period, with European countries falling one after another to the Germans and the retreat of the British Expeditionary Force from France.

In 1940 many people remember watching the Battle of Britain being fought out in the skies above in glorious weather.

Where possible memories have been matched with the relevant report in the Hambledon Air Raid Precautions Incident Books for 1940 -1945.

Dunkirk, May and June 1940

Heroic work was done by all sorts of little craft and people who rescued more than 30,000 troops from Dunkirk's shallow beaches and ferried them to larger ships under enemy fire. News filtered through. People went to see the troop trains at Shalford station and were very shocked at the state of the men.

Joan Dunn

We'd heard the news of the evacuation and were given permission during work to go down to Guildford Station. It was market day in North Street and the stallholders loaded us with fruit to take there. The soldiers in the trains were dirty and tired, some in an awful state with no shoes. The WVS and Salvation Army were giving out drinks. and lots of the soldiers were giving them letters to send to their loved ones to say they were safe, some proper letters, some just addresses on scraps of paper.

The Blitz

The Germans bombed London between September 1940 and May 1941

Bernard Hill

By 1940 the war really got underway with air raids a common occurrence. Fear was our biggest enemy from the drone of German aircraft en-route to and from London on many a night.

The sound of high explosive bombs going off, together with the tremors that shook the house all added to the tension.

The searchlight from the Gosden Common site regularly lit up the night sky as indeed did the brilliant red glow over Chinthurst Hill from the numerous fires in London. Even now one can quickly conjure up that awful drone of an enemy bomber passing overhead and the wailing sound of an air raid siren still gives one a cold shiver.

29th August 1940

Evelyn Nash

The first bomb that hit Bramley came down on Bramley Golf Course; there was no warning, we were woken by a loud thud which scared us all. We thought it was a bomb. There was some delay before it exploded at 6am and that time we were really frightened.

Everyone was up there the next day digging for souvenir bits. I didn't go up until after school and was jealous of boys like Ray Oliver who went up before school and found large lumps. Many children continued to collect shrapnel and spent bullets through the war.

Robin Hill

Dad was out with the Home Guard most nights but sometimes we were allowed briefly to stand outside and watch the glow as London burned in the Blitz. Air raid alerts were spent downstairs in the front room together, sometimes under the dining table, when things got a bit close.

24th September 1940

Three high explosive bombs came down at Nore.

Joy Perun and Joan Federchuk

Perce Radcliffe was coming from his home guard duties at Palmers Cross. The bomb had come down and the police were at one end of the lane stopping people go down. They forgot to seal off the other end and were very surprised when Perce arrived having cycled right over the area the unexploded bomb was in!

19th April 1941

Three high explosive and 200 incendiary bombs fell on the village. Many villagers remember this event. John Ives was evacuated to Bramley and heard the bombs go off in nearby Bramley Park, Nancy Smith recalls that army vehicles were also damaged there.

Bernard Hill

On the night of Saturday 19th April 1941 we had a shower of incendiary bombs which littered the area. These were small cylindrical bombs full of magnesium about 18 inches in length and about two inches in diameter. The fuse was in the nose which operated on impact. The ensuing fire was very difficult to put out as they would continue to burn under water. We had two incendiary bombs in our garden and lots fell along the river and canal bank which were extinguished with tuffets of grass. Fortunately none landed on anyone's roof.

Dick Turrell

The Germans came one night and dropped bombs in Bramley Park and Thorncombe Street. Surprisingly no one was hurt. Godfrey Stevens and I went out to Thorncombe Street to have a look. Mr Moller the owner came up to us and said "Would you like to earn half a crown?" "Yes, please, sir" we said. Mr Moller got two spades and we got digging. Four feet down we found the nose cap of the bomb. That was what Mr Moller wanted!

Evelyn Nash

A stick of incendiary bombs fell across the seven acres of Gosden Nursery. There were two wooden bungalows, several very large sheds, five large commercial greenhouses and all the cottages nearby on the Common, but the only damage was to a standard rose tree.

The collective Parsons family memories are mixed, Betty and Winnie (pictured opposite) slept through it all, Evelyn has a vivid memory of her father frantically shovelling earth over any he could find. There was a stirrup pump, but they were useless things and there was plenty of soil around. Next morning 52 burnt out cases were collected, one only a few feet from the house. Avis Day recalls that Gosden Common that night was as bright as day.

Other Bombs

There were nineteen other instances reported of bombs being dropped at Smithbrook, Nore Road, Primrose Way, Painshill Farm, Whipley Manor, Nurscombe, Tilsey Farm, Wintershall, Dane's Hole, near the Leathern Bottle and the railway cutting at Whipley Manor.

Over 250 bombs fell in the parish of Bramley mostly during August 1940 and June 1944, most of which fell between August 1940 and April 1941. In 1944 many flying bombs came into the area , but only one caused considerable damage.

Keith Jelley

I remember a barrage balloon which had broken loose and was dragging its cable. One day a boy picked up an incendiary bomb on the way to school and brought it into school. The teacher put it in a bucket of water!

John Hodgson

One night I was upstairs. It was a moonlit night and I could see the glow of the fires in London in the distance. I heard a noise which sounded like a plane slowly descending with engine stuttering. I looked towards Chinthurst Hill and saw the plane. It flew low over the house and I could plainly see the swastikas on the sides just before it crashed somewhere the other side of the Golf Course.

Peter Cansell

As a child I found the war both exciting and interesting. On many a fine night you could see aeroplanes everywhere and we used to watch the dog fights. Once a barrage balloon broke free and we saw it shot down by a Spitfire.

We used to walk along the ditch alongside the road on our way back from Bramley School. One day Ian Liddicott and I were walking along it and fell over something hard. With great difficulty we managed to uncover what turned out to be an incendiary bomb. We carried it home and put it on the doorstep of my house. When my mother saw it she nearly had a fit. So, we picked it up again and took it down to a house of a Policeman called Baxter and laid it on his doorstep. He nearly had a fit too. In next to no time the Canadians arrived from Bramley Park in a lorry with half a dozen men and took it away. We never heard of it again!

Brian Harms

We used to pick up scraps of aircraft, and also collected blanks, then threw them on a bonfire where they exploded.

The RAF used to do recovery with long lorries called 'Queen Mary's'. The drivers used to stop in Birtley Road and go into Bill's café. We boys used to swarm all over the vehicle picking up pieces of aeroplanes, particularly if they were German.

A British plane crashed at Lea Farm, Bramley on 30th July 1943

This was the second prototype Gloster E28/39 which was a flying test-bed for one of the revolutionary jet engines designed by Sir Frank Whittle. The pilot ran into difficulties after an aileron failure and bailed out.

Dick Turrell

One day I was working with Jack Horsfield in the fields. We all heard the roar, the aeroplane came down at Brookwell. We saw the pilot coming down in a parachute, one cord had got under his neck and he had to hold his head carefully so he did not get strangled. He came down in Wonersh and only broke his ankle. The plane had come down three fields from where we were working. We went over the fields to it, it was intact and not on fire and it had crashed with its nose pointing upwards. I noticed that it did not have a propeller. The Fire Service arrived and then the RAF came and guarded it. The next day it was loaded on to a trailer and carted away.

1st May 1944

A Royal Australian Air Force Halifax crashed at Upper Bonhurst

Aircraft

Halifax III LV 791 of 466 Squadron RAAF, 30th April - 1st May 1944 Leconfield

Crew

Capt F/L R J MacDermott, Air Bomber F/S W A Hines, Navigator F/S L T Saunders, W/O F/S T Evans, Rear Gunner F/S W V Dodd, Mid Upper Gunner F/S W S Shoemaker, F/Eng Sgt N M Brown

Target - Acheres

14 aircraft detailed to attack the target and returned safely, although captain of LV791 bailed crew out near Dunsfold and aircraft crashed as a result of damage. Primary attacked from 12,500 feet at 2354 hours.

Pilot's report

At approx 2215 mid upper gunner discovered that a piece of the front part of the fin approx 12' x 6" was torn and flapping. Pilot decided to continue as he did not think damage would extend. Aircraft was fully under control until approx 40 miles from our coast on return. For the rest of the journey almost completely out of control. Vibrating violently and alternately losing and gaining height. Pilot managed to get inland, crossing at Selsey Bill, and ordered crew to bale out from 8000' at approc 0100 hours. By this time the front part of the fin disappeared and pilot, after being thrown about and slightly burnt was eventually thrown clear and landed safely. F/S Evans had injured foot but remainder of crew were safe and unhurt.

Keith Jelley

I did not hear about this plane crash until a school friend, Peter Ragless, who lived at Bonhurst told me that a plane had crashed 150 yards from his home. It had been down for a few days when my father took me to see the wreckage. I remember walking along the wing and I collected the Perspex from the windows. We boys later made rings from these to wear on our fingers. Sometime in the last ten years I took a researcher to the site who found some pieces of the aircraft which had not been removed after it crashed.

Keith supplied the photograph and the report.

Peter Cansell

One night my younger brother and I were lying in bed and we heard a loud noise. We both scrambled to the window and saw an aeroplane coming straight towards us. It just cleared the top of the hill and then crashed at Bonhurst. Four or five of us went to see it and collected some rounds of ammunition. I remember it was getting towards harvest time and a week or two later we found a flying boot in the woods and then a logbook which we gave to PC Baxter. Later, when we were helping with the harvest, we found the other flying boot in the corn.

In June 1944 the Germans sent the first of the V1 flying bombs, known as doodlebugs, soon to be replaced by the deadlier V2 in September 1944.

16th August 1944

A flying bomb hit Cranleigh gasworks killing one person and injuring 22 others

Joy Perun

I remember running up to the front gate to meet my father. We both heard and saw a doodlebug very close to us. The engine stopped and my father threw me to the ground, my mother threw down the old dog "Badger" and lay on top of him. Then after a few seconds the engine started up again and the flying bomb moved away and eventually landed at Cranleigh Gasworks.

Cecily Taylor remembers a V1 which damaged Red Stream Cottage, Birtley on 8th July 1944

When the doodlebugs started it was mainly daytime. Then one night one dropped on the grass verge opposite the cottage at Birtley Green. It took the roof off the cottage. At the time it was owned and occupied by a Miss Finley Peacock. Miss Peacock, to do "her bit", worked in the grounds of Birtley House, which was occupied by Troughton and Young, electrical engineers working for the government on sites all over the country. Miss Peacock would turn up dressed in a woolly hat, and a voluminous old coat tied round the middle with string. She also wore heavy boots. On the night of the destruction she was out with a torch gathering debris for her fire. Quite unperturbed and back at work next day as usual. Other cottages, including ours, suffered superficial damage such as ceilings down and doors jammed. Luckily there was no loss of life.

Parish Magazine
Headmaster Mr E.J.Chapple.
August 1944

The C of E School broke up for the four week summer holiday on July 14th. We are not altogether sorry that the children were dispersed for a time and that they no longer had to listen for the doodlebugs approach. In this connection I should like to say a word of praise for the parents and the children. The parents for their part for sending the children to school, a little weary eyed sometimes, but they were there and the worst went on. As for the children they can have no nerves. The siren goes, the approach of the doodlebug is given and they dive for cover as though they had been at it for years. Two minutes later work is going on as usual. If the Germans wish to see what morale is like in England, let them see a school at work while the doodles dawdle over.

The last warning was on 4th March 1945. By this time the Allied Forces were well established in Europe and had destroyed all the rocket launching sites. Peace in Europe was declared on 8th May 1945.

TRAIN BOMBING

It was 2pm on Wednesday 16th December 1942 when the sirens went off. A lone Dornier appeared out of a dull, low December sky and dropped two high explosive bombs and then machine-gunned a train near Bramley Station. Seven people were killed including the driver and fireman, another person died later and 36 were injured, some quite seriously.

A full report including photographs was not published in the local papers until four years after the event due to wartime censorship.

Surrey Times & Weekly Press

21ˢᵗ December 1946
Badly Shaken Up

An eye witness account of this attack was given by Capt. F.U. Fargus, head warden of Bramley. It was a very wet afternoon and a very low cloud ceiling – about 500ft. I saw the bombs actually drop, and shortly afterwards there was a greenish light and a loud noise. We were badly shaken up.

The bomb which damaged the train was a 500lb. bomb dropped from low altitude. It first struck No. 1 Oakgate, and exploded by the railway fence as the two coach train came along. The train received the full blast, and the whole side was torn out, but the train miraculously remained upright on the rails. Flying glass injured most of the passengers. The driver and the guard, both Horsham men, were killed.

In that brief moment the orderliness of the vicinity was changed into a mass of rubble and debris. In what remained of the train, twisted bodies lay in the wreckage, tortured dazed people struggled onto the track and turned to assist those more injured than themselves.

The second 500lb. bomb struck the other side of the railway making a scoop in the earth. It ricocheted for 200 yards and finally struck Brook Grange, Gosden Common, and exploded. The occupants Mr. and Mrs. Braithwaite luckily escaped with minor cuts. They had finished lunch and left the dining room and were in the passage when the bomb went off. Though Mr. Braithwaite was knocked down by the blast, it was undoubtedly due only to the fact they were in the passage that saved their lives. The whole wing of the house was demolished.

It was thought by officials that two unexploded bombs had fallen, and the orders were given for the evacuation of the houses around Oakgate. [There were several houses with gardens that went down to the railway line called Oakgate Cottages in the last section of Eastwood Road.] Whilst this was in progress an inspection was made by the Army Bomb Disposal Unit, and the evacuation was called off.

BROOK GRANGE, BRAMLEY, demolished in the same incident, the house in which Mr. and Mrs. Braithwaite both had lucky escapes from death, and emerged with scratches.   [*Photo: W. Dennell, Guildford.*]

Memories of those on the train

Paul Leaney was a ten week old baby travelling on the train with his mother

On December 16th 1942, Rita Leaney travelled by train to Farnborough, where her husband was on standby with the Tank Corps for embarkation to North Africa and had not seen their ten-week-old son.

On her return journey from Guildford that afternoon, a lone Dornier 217 Bomber descended from the clouds looking for an opportunist target as the train was approaching Bramley Station. It was bombed and strafed by machine guns, killing seven and injuring many more. The raider was shortly afterwards pursued by a Beaufighter over the coast and crashed into a gasometer at Bognor killing the four crew members.

Rita was struck in the side of the face by a bullet, which shattered her jawbone and exited from the opposite temple taking out an eye. She also had deep penetration wounds from the glass from the shattered windows. Her son Paul also had glass wounds and she remembered passing him down from the wrecked carriage to a Canadian soldier who helped her on foot along to the station. She was taken to Park Prewitt Hospital at Basingstoke, where she found herself laying in a dingy cell with a small barred window that was made to house 19th century lunatics.

She was later transferred to East Grinstead for operations by Alexander Macindoe, the celebrated plastic surgeon. This was followed by a long period of convalescence at Shoreham. Paul was looked after by grandparents for 2 years at Rudgwick. She was very philosophical about her fate and didn't blame anyone, considering herself lucky; the woman who had been next to her on the train was killed and she remembered the other patients at East Grinstead, mostly burnt airmen who had lost their faces and their eyesight and still kept a sense of humour. She had a successful business in Horsham and in Billingshurst, and died in 1997.

Ruth Bailey

I was comfortably knitting, pleased that I had nearly finished my Christmas present for my mother, when as we slowed down on our approach to Bramley Station, I suddenly heard machine gunfire hitting the train. On looking up I had a fleeting glimpse of the plane, out of the window, flying in the direction of Guildford. It was very low, just above the trees. Then there was a big explosion and the train rocked on the rails, but fortunately did not go over. The door on the far side was blown out and the glass from the windows flew across the compartment. I realised at once what had happened, but then everything went completely quiet and still. I suppose, because I was young my reactions were quick. I got my hands over my face before the glass blew in and had no bad damage done to my face, only nicks, although my hands were cut. Many people were not so lucky and had bad facial injuries, several losing eyes. I can remember getting up off the seat and feeling blood running down my face from cuts on my head and ear and thinking "Well, I am still alive."

As the door of the compartment had blown out of the train I was able to jump down out of the train onto the grass verge, other passengers were emerging too. Someone called to me from the first coach, the one nearest the engine, asking me to go round to the other side of the train to help them with an injured passenger. To get to them I had to go round behind the engine and along the embankment on the far side of the train. It was much steeper on that side but I was able to scramble along it. There was a man lying on the ground, quite still, and I imagine he had been blown out of the train. I couldn't stop to look at him as I was being called from the train by the man who had originally spotted me. They handed me a very young baby asking me to take it to safety somewhere, as the mother was badly injured. I took the baby, which seemed unhurt except for a small cut on the end of its nose. I supposed its mother was hurt protecting it from the flying glass and was unable to protect herself in any way. I thought the best thing to do was to take the baby to the station where there was sure to be someone to help.

A little way down the line I saw people leaning over a fence looking along the railway line to see what happened. One of them promised to look after the baby so I handed it over to them to care for. On returning to the train I found some Canadian soldiers doing great work in getting the injured out of the train and administering First Aid. One passenger I noticed was a soldier who had been propped up against the fence, pouring blood from a wound in his neck and shaking like a leaf. He also looked as if he had bad injuries to his eyes. A Canadian soldier said he could take him to hospital in his jeep if he could get him to the road. We tried to stop the bleeding making a pressure pad with a handkerchief, but it did not do much good. We then pulled a seat out of the train to make a kind of stretcher and covered him up with a coat to keep him warm. By this time the ambulances were beginning to arrive, and I don't know what happened to him after that, except that he was still alive in a hospital ward the next day. It was only then that I noticed that I had a deep cut on my knee and it was obvious that it was going to need stitching. I was not aware of anything hurting , just lots of blood everywhere. In Eastwood Road a Canadian soldier sitting in a jeep said he would take me to hospital if I liked, so I went with him.

In 2006 Bramley History Society made it possible for Paul and Ruth to meet again. They discovered that both Paul's mother and Ruth had, for many years, received a Christmas card signed 'from a Canadian soldier'.

Memories of those who lived in Eastwood Road

Russell Hudson

I was just six years old; my aunt had picked me up from Miss Smith's infants class at the end of the school day. During the day the class had all got under the desks, after the air raid siren had sounded. Little did I realise what had happened to the train and its passengers and the lower part of Eastwood Road.

As we approached the station and Eastwood Road there was a lot of activity; the lower section of Eastwood Road resembled what I imagined a battlefield was like. One bomb had 'bounced' through one side of number 93 and out the other side, carrying on through the rear gardens, finally exploding on the boundary of number 119 and and 121 with the railway fence. Fortunately no one was killed through this particular bomb, although Mrs Clue in bungalow number 121 had a few cuts and was rather shaken up. The only fatality was a goldfish. There was serious damage to the roofs and windows to numbers 119 and 121. We moved to Shalford to my grandfather's house for several months whilst the war damage contractors repaired ours and the other adjacent houses.

Doris Porter by her daughter Bev Callow

Doris Porter lived at Eastwood Road. She was at home when the train was bombed at Bramley Station. She heard children crying and as she had easy access to the railway line she rushed out to help, being one of the first people to get there. She then took some of the children into her home including a baby, and looked after them.

Bev has a badge which her mother mounted on black velvet that was given her at the time of the bombing. We do not know who gave the badge to her but it appears to be a soldier's hat badge.

Geoffrey Knapp

I was working for Westminster Wines and it was my afternoon off. I was with my mother in our garden when I heard a plane flying very low. I ran to the side of the house and could see it was a German plane and I saw it drop two bombs. I shouted to my mother to get down but she tried to run into the house and was cut on the arm by flying glass as our window exploded in the blast. I got my mother's arm tied up and shovelled up most of the glass. When I got to the train they were bringing out the dead and laying them along the grass banks.

Angela Harms

I lived with my parents at 75 Eastwood Road, two houses away from the railway line. On the day the train was bombed, when I was five or six years old, I was off sick from Bramley School and at home with my mother.

We were both standing in the pantry when the air raid siren went off. My mother rushed me into the cupboard under the stairs. We then heard a terrific crash. My mother then ran out of the house. She returned and ushered me into the front room. I can remember somebody telling me not to look out, but I peeped out behind the curtains and could see people being brought up the front path into our house. I can remember a soldier with his ear hanging off, and amongst two or three others, a baby was brought into the house. My mother looked after them and coped magnificently but was upset and troubled by this.

Georgina Harvey

The day the train was bombed I was walking back to the MHH with my friend Jean Bartlett. We were between Eastwood Road and the field. It was a misty day with drizzly rain. We saw the aeroplane flying very low. We heard the machine gun fire and the bombs exploding. We watched one go through the bedroom of the house adjoining Mrs Barnard's house and then bounce into the road in front of the Shrubbs Cottages. It took out the windows and the roof was damaged.

We were the first people to get to the train. We could do very little. I remember the train had been split lengthwise. The Canadian soldiers were very quick coming down from Chinthurst Hill. Then the police arrived and we were quickly moved on. I went back into my home. When the police found me in the house they told me to go to the Jolly Farmer where everybody else was sent. They did however allow me to stay until my husband came home from work. When he did, we went and stayed the night with his parents in Chilworth. The police watched our house. They put tarpaulins on the roof and boarded up the windows.

Other Childrens' Memories

Bernard Hill

We were sitting in class at Bramley School. It was about a quarter to two in the afternoon. The Rev Selby-Lowndes was teaching us scripture at the time. When the siren went we were told to get under our desks. I remember the Vicar put his head in a waste paper basket. When we were allowed out of school we went out and picked up mementoes.

Sally Caton

She was seven years old at the time of the bombing, and attended St Martha's School. She wrote the letter below to an Aunt.

"The Owls nest",
Dear nora.
I hope Elisebeth likes the book. and the one Daddy sent her. We brak up on the 22 of Desber. and I am Glad that We are at Last.
I hope you will have a happy xmas.
I got such shoke the other day at school and if we went out for a walk we woeaed of ten cort but it was a wet day. so we had to stay in

there was such a bang we all thoghe it was. Thunder. but it was a bome. very near. to us. but it was much more near to the little Gosden it was opesite to them.
It was the brithcata weneend I have to go over but acose the morning. I made a fuse this moring. When mummy came over I acaed her. if she woeued come over with me.

To see it and she seid she aroued. so we went over. Well you shoud see the site. the trees look so furey. the curtams. which haning in hedgees and trees the gences. windos panes are broker en the comon look relly drefully. well you ought come and see it. wishing you a happy xmas. with lots of love from Sally. M.

Ula Oakley

I remember I had been home to lunch at Linersh Wood. My father and I were walking along Barton Road when a plane flew very low overhead. My father later said he saw the bombs being released. He hurried me along. I remember the level crossing gates were open and when we arrived at St Catherine's School everybody was sitting in the downstairs corridors. I was not aware that the train had been bombed until later. My piano teacher's sister Alice Fortune who had attended St Catherine's School was killed; she was a talented cellist and was returning home to Cranleigh from London.

Richard Moore

Soon after lunch we heard the throbbing drone of a low flying German aircraft, followed shortly afterwards by the unmistakable crump, crump of two or three bombs exploding. We lived over my father's business, the village pharmacy.

At around the same time a Canadian Army convoy was passing through the village, and a number of vehicles, including ambulances, were seen to divert towards the railway station. My mother being in the Red Cross set off on foot immediately to give assistance, followed by my father, who always had a shoulder bag of dressings etc. at the ready in case of just such an emergency. He was slower on his feet, being lame as a result of Great War injuries. As a 12 or 13 year old boy, I had no desire to remain in the property alone, so cycled round to the railway, where I carried bandages and other first aid dressings between helpers. Apart from military personnel, a number of local people, including Dr. James Paterson, had gone to give assistance.

A report from The Manitoba Dragoons War diary
December 1942

In the Field 16th Dec.

14.50 hrs. Lone German raiding plane dropped bombs on Bramley Station vicinity today (449645) Bomb damage done to a train approaching the station from Guildford and houses nearby. Eight people died in the wreckage about 25 more were injured. Valiant work was done by those rendering first aid by the men of D Squadron, RHQ, and C Squadron.

In the Field 17th Dec.

As a result of the low level bombing in Bramley yesterday: our troops are ordered to carry filled magazines on their Brent in the race cars when out training.

In the Field 18th Dec.

Squad of 12 men under Lieut. E.D.Morgan worked all day cleaning up the debris in one of the houses bombed on 16th December. They reported great temptation to become "looters" on finding three "Purdy" shotguns in the ruins.

This is confirmed by H77571 Trooper Herb M. Schuppert pictured opposite.

As I was in "D" Squadron I was in Bramley Park. If not doing Staghound training I relieved the duty and dispatch riders while they went on leave for something to do other than general fatigue jobs which were not my favorite. I was in Bramley the day the Stuka Dive Bomber (sic) hit the train and station and seen all the commotion. There were a couple of us and we went to give whatever aid we could.

Reports from further afield

George Carter

I was working as a milkman for Mr Grist. I was near Luxford's Garage in Birtley Road when the air raid siren went off. It was around a quarter past two in the afternoon and I saw a large aeroplane flying along the railway line in the Guildford direction. I knew it was a German bomber by the noise it made. I took cover between two houses. I saw the door of the plane open and three bombs fell out about where Bramley Station was. I tried to get to the site that had been bombed but was unable to do so because there were so many Canadian troops coming down Snowdenham Lane and going down Station Road. Later I went down Eastwood Road. I saw the house where the bomb had gone into the upstairs bedroom and out the other side whilst the lady downstairs was completely unharmed. I knew another woman who lived down there who was very upset as the troops had brought dead bodies into her house and laid them on her table.

Evelyn Nash

I saw nothing of the plane that dropped the bombs on the train. Then a messenger came to say my mother Mary Parsons, had been injured by flying glass. I went home to my grandfather's cottage on Gosden Common. My sister Betty and sister-in-law Winnie arrived back from work, wet through, but we weren't allowed to go up to our bungalow, as there was glass everywhere.

I still wasn't really upset, but reality sunk in when my father and I went to the Royal Surrey Hospital to visit my mother. She was lying there all grey and shrunken, with bandages round her neck. A splinter of glass had just missed her jugular vein. Otherwise she was unharmed, though badly shocked. She had to stay in hospital over Christmas. My brother was home on embarkation leave, and she said afterwards that she cried herself to sleep on Christmas Eve.

Doris Bothamley, my mother's cousin, hastily cycled round to the Nursery to see if everyone was safe. She found her bleeding heavily, and her husband in a state of shock. Doris rushed to the main road and flagged down a Canadian Army lorry and got the driver to take her to hospital.

Betty Browne and Winnie Parsons remember 'cleaning up great piles of glass and washing floors, etc., laughing one minute, crying the next and with the added worry that Mum was so ill.'

Arthur Dunn

My father was working in the garden of the Braithwaite's house on Gosden Common. Two bombs ricocheted over the lawns, off the roof of the house and then off the roof of a cottage on the other side of the Common in Tannery Lane. A family called Mears lived there. My father was flung into the bushes.

Dorothy Booth

Some people must remember that a bomb fell at Gosden Common, completely demolishing a lovely house opposite Gosden. No one was in during a daylight raid, but we were appalled to return from Guildford County School to the school at Gosden, to find the house was gone. There had been a warning siren in the afternoon and the school went down to the shelters. I vividly remember piano keys in the grass of the Common, and rags, pieces of fabric fluttering in telephone wires. If the staff remaining at Gosden that day were shattered and shocked, they didn't show it. Lots of sangfroid and an amazing escape for Gosden House. The German plane went from Bramley to Guildford via Shalford.

Mike Laws

I attended a school at Wonersh during the war. It was about two fifteen in the afternoon. We were in the Shalford Scout Hut doing woodwork. We heard some loud noises and we all rushed to the windows, which were covered with wire netting. At that time there was not much vegetation growing alongside the railway line and we could see the German plane flying low above the line. We were told to come away from the windows immediately. My mother was in Guildford shopping at the time and saw the plane flying above Guildford and dived for cover in a shop doorway.

John May

Walking down towards Guildford, just about where the top end of Wodeland Avenue meets the Farnham Road by the allotments, I was suddenly frightened by the noise of aeroplane engines and machine gun fire. I fell to the pavement on my face and remember seeing the 'plane fly over the hospital and the County School for Girls. I was unhurt but for many years later began to wonder whether the whole episode was a figment of a schoolboy's imagination - not so - I know, because I was there!

THE WRECKED TRAIN. — Exclusive pictures of the wrecked train at Bramley, after the side had been blown out by a German bomb on December 16th, 1942. Eight people were killed and 40 injured.

The photograph above, from the Surrey Advertiser 21st December 1946, shows the train where it came to rest, with St. Catherines and the old goods yard visible in the background. It was near the far end of Eastwood Road when it was hit. The local newspaper reported this to have been the worst bombing incident in the Guildford district during the war.

THOSE REMEMBERED

Those who gave their lives

Bramley War Memorial & Cemetery

SERGEANT REGINALD DONALD ADGEY-EDGAR

Intelligence Corps

Died in 1944 aged 29, is buried in Bramley Cemetery

MAJOR RAYMOND BEENEY

Royal Engineers

Died in 1943 aged 32, is buried at La Reunion Cemetery in France

PRIVATE LESLIE CANSELL

The Queen's Royal Regiment

Died in 1944 aged 31, is buried at the Mook War Cemetery, Netherlands

LIEUTENANT PETER CANTI

Royal Engineers

Died in 1944 aged 31, is buried in Kirkee War Cemetery India

SAPPER GEORGE HARBROE

Royal Engineers

Died in 1940 aged 26, is buried in Bramley Cemetery

LIEUTENANT COMMANDER PATRICK HAVERS

Royal Navy

Died in 1943 aged 35, his name is on the Lee-on-Solent Memorial

TELEGRAPHIST ALLEN HEARSEY

Royal Navy

Died in 1941 aged 20 when his ship H.M.S.Barham was torpedoed and sank off Egypt, his name is
on the Portsmouth War Memorial

LANCE CORPORAL ALBERT HOOK

The Queen's Royal Regiment

Died in 1943 aged 21, is buried at Salerno War Cemetery, Italy

CAPTAIN FREDERICK KAHL

Royal Fusiliers

Died in 1942 aged 32 whilst training as a commando in North Wales, is buried in Brookwood
Cemetery

SAPPER JAMES KINSELLA

Royal Engineers

Died in 1944 aged 43, is buried in Bramley Cemetery, but his name is not on the Bramley War
Memorial

LANCE CORPORAL WALTER MILLER
The Queen's Royal Regiment
Died in 1945 aged 26, is buried at Forli War Cemetery, Italy

LIEUTENANT-COMMANDER RALPH NORRIS
R.N.V.R.
Died in 1945 aged 27, his name is on the Lee-on-Solent War Memorial

PRIVATE SIDNEY NORTH
R.A.M.C.
Died in 1941 aged 21, is buried in Bramley Cemetery

AIRCRAFTMAN 1ST CLASS R.S.ST. RAYMOND WHITBOURN
Royal Air Force
Died in 1942 aged 20 is buried in Bramley Cemetery

LANCE CORPORAL JOHN WILD
East Surreys
Died in 1940 aged 33, his name is on the Dunkirk Memorial

PRIVATE FREDERICK WILLIAMSON
The Queen's Royal Regiment
Died in 1941 aged 25, is buried in Bramley Cemetery

RICHARD WOOD
Royal Irish Fusiliers
Died in 1943 aged 27, is buried at the Sangro River War Cemetery, Italy

Grafham War Memorial
LANCE CORPORAL CECIL JOHN NAPPER
1st Btn Devonshire Regiment No 6089214
Died in 1944 aged 32, is buried at Imphal cemetery North East India, Grave Ref 4d H

On the right hand side of the Church wall by the entrance door is a stone memorial set into the wall with World War 1 names. Lance Corporal C Napper's name has been added at the bottom.

Holy Trinity Church
The Sanctuary lamp is a memorial to Reginald Adgey-Edgar who died in 1942. Later, his parents also donated the golden angel on top of Guildford Cathedral.

Avis Day
My stepfather James Penny, was brought back from Italy having lost an arm, my brother Raymond came back also. D-Day has memories for me, my twenty first birthday; I still have a 21 page letter my brother wrote whilst in Italy. War is not funny, Billy Turrell the boy next door, came home minus a leg, Bertie Hook and Ray Whitbourne lost their lives, Gordon Carpenter lost an arm, all youths from the same class at school, how very sad, what a waste of young lives.

Peter Cansell

I do not remember the beginning of the war. My father was Leslie James Cansell who, before war started worked, as a slaughter man at Grinstead's in Bramley. He joined the Queen's Royal Regiment. I do not remember him leaving home. I remember him coming home on leave and I have a photograph of him and my younger brother sitting in his army vehicle. He was killed in Holland on 23rd November 1944. It was dark when the telegram came six days later on 29th November. My mother's father was with us at the time. My mother was very shocked. Then life went on as usual.

Jim Hook

My younger brother Albert worked as a carpenter's apprentice at Robinsons the builders in Guildford before the war. I last saw him when I joined the RAF in 1940. I was in Naples when my parents wrote to say my brother had been killed. I had last seen him in 1940, three years previously. I was on leave at the time and made my way to the graveyard in Salerno where he was buried. I did not even have to look for the grave, I found it immediately. I took a photograph of it. Since then my nephew, who never knew his father and who was 18 months old when he died, has been there and taken another picture of his grave, now like the others with headstone and flowers planted at the base.

The late David Elliott

We had one fatality in Grafham, L. Corp. Napper was knocked down by a lorry out in the Far East. After the war we decided we must have a war memorial. We thought it would be a nice idea to put up two bus shelters. We sent the appeal out and all the people put in their £5 and £1 notes. We raised the money and the shelters had little plaques on them, which were soon stolen by people as souvenirs.

Guy Selby-Lowndes

My sister Alison was the eldest child of my parents. After graduating from Kings College, London, she learned secretarial skills. Her work was always based in London, where she lodged in Paddington. One night when making her way home in the blackout she walked into a bollard and fell. Initially her injuries were thought to be minor, but abdominal pains developed and it was discovered that her internal organs had been ruptured. She was operated on twice at the Royal Surrey Hospital, but died of secondary shock. She is interred in Bramley Cemetery.

THE AUSTERE PEACE

Bramley was an optimistic place, and set up a Peace Commemoration committee in May 1945. The committee included all the people who had been so busy organising the war effort.

Peace Commemoration Plans

The minutes of their meeting were preserved in the Parish Council safe, and are now in the Bramley History Society's archives.

After much discussion, six possible projects were listed,

1. A new organ for the church
2. A holiday home by the sea.
3. A recreation ground.
4. A village hall and recreation ground.
5. A new village hall.
6. Improvements to the existing village hall.

Events were held to raise money, and finally the funds were spent on the War Memorial, refurbishment of the Village Hall, and the levelling of Gosden Common to create a cricket pitch alongside the established football pitch.

All returning Service people and war widows were given a sum of money.

VE Day - Victory in Europe - 8th May 1945

The Bramley church bells rang seven hundred and twenty Grandsire doubles. Street parties and bonfires were organised on VE Day. At Chestnut Way an enormous bonfire was built in the field where the Range is now. In Snowdenham Lane Barbara Gall remembers that tables and chairs were put out in

Springfield Terrace. Flags were put up and paper hats worn. It was a lot of fun, parents made jellies, cakes and sandwiches.

In Eastwood Road, Georgina Harvey remembers making a cake for a street party in Eastwood Road (pictured opposite) and in Birtley Rise, Jean Hopwood remembers great celebration round a bonfire in the garden next to the Vicarage.

Brian Harmes

There was dancing in Bramley High Street. We had a bonfire at Chestnut Way. We had some rook scarers from a farm which we put in a milk churn. This was in lieu of fireworks, and we waited for the bang!

Patricia Blythman

My father helped organise the Hurst Hill bonfire. My Mum went down to the Wheatsheaf where they were playing the piano outside. I remember a Canadian soldier walking us children home, and he pushed my youngest brother in the pram.

Peter Cansell

We scoured the woods for wood, and we helped build the bonfire. Everybody at Hurst Hill pooled their foodstuffs and we had a street party.

David Hooper

On VE Day we all went into Guildford by car, and were driving down the High Street, which was very crowded, when I saw someone strike a thunder flash and throw it in our direction. I couldn't see where it went, but when it exploded - they were very powerful - I realised it had been on the car roof. The sliding roof panel was open, and we had a very near miss, as it would have hit my mother if it had dropped in. In a time of peace that was actually more dangerous than anything we had experienced during the previous five years of war.

Richard Moore

I remember VE Day. My mother, who was in the Red Cross, was at Dunsfold helping to re-patriate prisoners of war.

I took a bus to Guildford. There was dancing and music and streamers and fireworks in the High Street. Despite the cobbles we managed a conga. I had to walk home afterwards.

Dick Turrell

I went to work as usual, but also went down the pub. On the Saturday we were still celebrating in the Wheatsheaf. Pints of beer were poured into the piano. This was played at weekends by Mrs Burrell. Dick Richardson and a mate stripped down, dried and cleaned the piano so it was in working order for Sunday evening.

Surrey Advertiser
12th May 1945

The Rev. D.G. Legg (vicar) officiated at a largely attended V.E. Day service at Bramley parish church on Tuesday. There was a service at Grafham, with the Rev. Harris (curate) officiating.

From loudspeakers in the High Street arranged by Mr Robertson many heard the King's speech and on that night and the next night there was dancing.

A bonfire was lighted at Birtley. Tomorrow (Sunday) there is a Thanksgiving service.

The Peace

VJ Day - Victory in Japan - 15th August 1945

News from that sphere of conflict had been sparse. Many of the Servicemen there called themselves 'The Forgotten Army'.

Jean Hopwood

I remember VJ Day and realising that the war was finally over. We were in Clacton at the time, having our first family holiday since the beginning of the war.

The Peace saw no easing of rationing, in fact things got worse, with some allowances diminished, and bread rationed. The country was practically bankrupt, and many luxury goods, including spirits, were being exported to earn all-important dollars.

There was a scarcity of building materials, and a great housing shortage when returning service men married, and those married in the war sought their own homes.

Betty Browne

Harry and I were married on 13th October 1945 in Holy Trinity Church. Rationing was still on so it was hard to buy goods. My wedding dress was bought in Guildford High Street. It was the only one that fitted me, so there wasn't any choice. We managed to obtain lace gloves and a veil. The bridesmaids' dresses were borrowed. Our reception was held in the Bramley Village Hall, it was the first time the hall had been available since before the war. Food was prepared by family, friends and neighbours who all shared their rations.

But while the adults were struggling with shortages and changing domestic situations, life was suddenly wonderful for the teenagers. The Youth Club was expanded and met in various venues, St. Catherine's, St. Faith's, the little hall and also two large rooms in Bramley Park. There were discussions, quizzes, outside speakers, ballroom and country dancing, table tennis and board games.

Ivy Durrant

I must have learnt about the Bramley Youth Club from Jean Vestage. I used to cycle down from the bottom of Winkworth Hollow, through Thorncombe Street and down Snowdenham Lane. My mother never seemed worried about me going down the dark lonely lanes, her only words as I left were 'Now you be home by 10!'

We had two rooms for general activities at Bramley Park, but I especially remember the ballroom dancing classes held in St. Catherine's Speech Hall run by Miss Kilburn. She was an excellent teacher, didn't put up with any nonsense, and we were quite willing to be taught, I can't remember anyone misbehaving.

Groups from the Youth Club helped with painting work during the refurbishment of the Village Hall.

Victory Day - 8th June 1946

A public holiday was declared with local parades and general celebrations. Bramley Athletic Club organised a Victory Day Gala

Surrey Advertiser
BRAMLEY'S PEACE
CELEBRATIONS
15th June 1946

A commemorative beaker was presented to each child taking part in the Victory Celebrations at Bramley, which owing to the weather were spread over two days. The proceedings organised by Bramley Athletic Club, began with a fancy dress parade from Gosden Common to Bramley Park via the High street.

The procession was led by the newly-formed Bramley Novelty Band. On arrival at the sports field, a heavy downpour drove everybody into the marquees where the dresses were judged. An attempt to hold the sports was abandoned, and the programme was postponed until Monday. It was possible however, to give tea to the children and pensioners in the marquees and a happy time was spent.

On Monday the weather, although dull, did not prevent a sports programme of 36 events being carried out, and the side shows were well patronised

8th June, 1946

TO-DAY, AS WE CELEBRATE VICTORY, I send this personal message to you and all other boys and girls at school. For you have shared in the hardships and dangers of a total war and you have shared no less in the triumph of the Allied Nations.

I know you will always feel proud to belong to a country which was capable of such supreme effort; proud, too, of parents and elder brothers and sisters who by their courage, endurance and enterprise brought victory. May these qualities be yours as you grow up and join in the common effort to establish among the nations of the world unity and peace.

George R.I.

Hazel Mulkeirins

I remember being in the fancy dress parade with my younger brother Guy. Our mother had made us both wigs from wool. Guy had his face blackened and was dressed as a "Robertson's jam golliwog". I also wore a wig. I had a jacket with a waistcoat over a white blouse with a lace jabot, knickerbockers with white stockings with my school shoes with cardboard buckles on them. I remember the Bramley Novelty Band. Most people in it seemed to play the kazoo.

John Brown

I remember the sports on Gosden Common on Victory Day. I won a first prize in one race and came second in another. I was given a commemorative beaker.

Food from South Africa

Extracts from the Parish Council Meetings show that shortages continued, and foodstuffs were being sent from South Africa.

Bramley Parish Council Minute Book
28th August 1946

The Clerk reported that he received 5 cases of sausages, 1 case of jam, 1 case of peaches, and 1 case of cheese (228 tins) from Hambledon Rural District Council as a gift from the People of South Africa. These gifts the council decided to give away in early December.

Troops coming home

Ron Hill

There was no leave possible for troops serving in the Middle East. Accordingly we were away from home for up to four years. By 1944 the Mediterranean was made safe enough for some to have home leave. The numbers were too big for everyone to come so all eligible soldiers' names were entered into a lottery entitled 'Leave in Advance of Python'. I was lucky to be selected.

Coming home to Bramley, whilst a pleasure, was an education to us into the tribulations all our families had been experiencing at home whilst we were overseas. It was when I was home on leave the news of the dropping of the first atomic bombs on Japan precipitated the Japanese capitulation and the end of hostilities.

Python was the code name for the demobilisation procedure from 1946. To avoid repeating the problems that arose after the end of World War I with unregulated demobilisation, every serviceman was placed in a numbered group, based on the length of war service. It was efficient and fair. My group was number 25. On leaving the army we were each provided with a civilian suit, raincoat, a trilby hat and other clothing and we had a ration book for the first time.

Doug Realff

I was with the 14th Army in Burma. I came back to England by boat in 1946; I was then a staff sergeant. I was disgusted, there was nobody there to meet us, no music, no nothing, just ration books. The war in Europe was well passed. I only had a uniform of jungle greens and a bush hat; they were the only clothes I had. To be demobbed I went to Great Ayton in Yorkshire. We were parading and a young officer of about twenty-three said to me "Go and take that poncy uniform off", I was somewhat angry. We were then given civilian clothes.

Alfred Haygarth

In 1945 I returned home by boat. The sick and wounded were flown back. I had three months service left to do. I was posted to St Luke's Hospital, Guildford, that was partly a military hospital. When army personnel were ready to leave hospital I used to take them up to Stoughton Barracks for a medical and for them to complete the paperwork. I also used to collect the mens' supplies of cigarettes and chocolates. I used to add a few to the numbers and give the extra to the nurses when they came off duty.

I met my wife who was a nurse there. When I was demobbed I did not return home to Lancashire. I found work in the Guildford area and married in 1946.

Roger Thoday

I joined the RAF as a volunteer at the beginning of the war. I served in many places. I was demobbed in 1946 and nothing much seemed to have changed. Like the other Bramley servicemen I was given ten shillings (50p). Opposite our house, Wharf Cottage, used to be a sign by the telephone post with the words 'unexploded bomb'. I never knew if this was true or whether it was put up to keep people off that piece of land!

Brian Avery

I was not demobbed until Christmas 1946. I went to Northolt for twenty-four hours for this. For the first time all ranks slept together in the same room in the barracks. Some were the worse for drink and when lights were out continued making a noise. An orderly came and told us off but hastily retreated when he was addressed by one of our number who was a very senior officer.

Jim Hook

I came home to Bramley in 1946 having been away for four and a half years. Nothing much seemed to have changed. I remember being taken to the Wheatsheaf for the evening I came home and beer was 4d (2p) a pint. I settled down to civilian life quickly. Food was tight and we ate better in the forces.

Finding work

The pre-war jobs of many men had been kept open for them as they returned home. The women were no longer needed to work in factories and on the land and in other jobs previously done by men. They were expected to settle back staying at home being just housewives and mothers. Many men found it difficult to find work and often earnings were less than they were during the war years.

Doug Realff

I had to go back to Bramley as that was where I was working before war started. Luckily for me the Shalford Nursery I had worked for was closing down and I would no longer be needed. The village barber told me that they were looking for people to work at Dunsfold Aerodrome. After the war Dunsfold created new jobs and employed a lot of people from this area.

Betty Brockman

My father was on the night shifts at the MHH so had to sleep during the day. He earned £4 at the factory, he'd never been so well paid in all his life! After he'd been released from the Directed Labour Scheme, he went back to the Bramley C of E School and earned £2 10s (£2.50) again.

Beryl Freeman

My brother Stephen Hubbard was a boot and shoe repairer. He was called up and sent to Italy to make boots for soldiers with deformed feet. When he came back in 1945 I remember he was very restless. Things had changed, people were wearing wellington boots in the winter and sandals in the summer and the demand for his skills had lessened and he sought other work.

Housing Shortage

Bramley Parish Council Minute Book

28th August 1946

The Clerk was instructed to inform the Hambledon Rural District that the Council was not in favour of the site at Woodrough Lane for council houses as it faced north and has a belt of trees on the south side and that there was very little sun, as an alternative site the council suggested that the chestnut patch behind the council houses in Hurst Hill.

Many young couples were living with their parents. Hambledon Rural District Council began building houses, first an extension to Chestnut Way, and then in The Coombes, on land that had in part been the school garden. Several old cottages in Woodrough Lane were swept away in the process.

Doug Realff

My wife, son and I were living with my parents in Birtley Rise so needed larger accommodation. We went to the Council. They had just put up six 'prefabs' at the Range. They said as I was an exserviceman I could have one. It was very comfortable with two large bedrooms, a living room, and a modern kitchen with a refrigerator.

Betty Browne

There were six of us, including a baby in a two bedroomed bungalow. Harry and I were allocated a three bedroomed house in Chestnut Way. Other young village couples became our neighbours.

In the 1951 census the population of Bramley was 2914.

Parish Magazine
December 1947
From the Vicar's letter

My dear people,

In these days we are constantly being reminded of shortages in many of the things we really enjoyed before the war and are now severely rationed. We are told by those in authority that it may take some time to free us from these restrictions.

Rationing timetable

Items	First Rationed	De-rationed
Tea	1940	1952
Sugar	1940	1953
Cream	1940	1953
Butter	1940	1954
Meat	1940	1954
Petrol	1939	1950
Shell eggs	1941	1953
Cheese	1941	1954
Clothes	1941	1949
Jam	1941	1948
Sweets	1942	1953
Bread	1946	1948

Bramley after the war

Very slowly life got back to normal, sports clubs revived, new societies were founded and consumer choice gradually returned.

The Bramley of 2007 is very different from that of 60 years ago, but a lot of the old still remains both in memory and in memorabilia. The research for this book has aroused much interest in things long put aside, and brought about rewarding reunions.

The A281 is now clogged with commercial traffic instead of military vehicles. Some things change, some stay the same. However, Bramley is still very much a community just as it was during the dark days of the Second World War.

ACKNOWLEDGEMENTS

Cranleigh and South Eastern Agricultural Society

David Elliott's book - 50 Not Out

Manitoba Dragoons

Gord Sim, secretary and the staff of 26 Field Regiment XII Manitoba Dragoons Museum, Brandon, Manitoba, Canada. Visit their on line museum at www.12mbdragoons.com

Schools

Mrs A.M.Phillips St Catherine's School and Mrs Elisabeth Reed

Mrs A. Champness Bramley Church of England Infant School

Surrey Advertiser

For various newspaper articles and to David Rose for his help and advice

Surrey Federation of Womens Institutes

Surrey: Within Living Memory

Surrey History Service ©

Reproduced with their permission

Bramley Parish Magazines October 1943 - June 1947 Ref; 6547/11/ box 1

Bramley Civil Parish Records Minute Book 1941-1958. Ref; 59/5/3

Hambledon Air Raid precautions Incident Books for 1940-1945. Surrey History services Ref; 6979/2/ 1 and 2

Illustrations

Avis Day - Works Pass 33

Basil Blythman - Drawing from "The Smallholding" 14

Bernard Hill

    One of a set of 55 aircraft silhouettes from Sweet Caporal cigarette packets 55

    Book Drive 43

Bev Callow - Hat pin given to her mother 70

Bramley History Society

    Bramley Park 56

    Bramley Juvenile orchestra in the "small hall" 45

    Bramley Wartime Police 7

    Dance Poster 39

    Dos and Don'ts 19

    Gym class 51

    Invasion poster 30

    MHH staff photograph 32

    School clock 50

    Woodrough House 23

Cecily Taylor - G Company 5th Batallion Home Guard 24

Charlie Palmer
    1ST Wonersh and Bramley Wolf Cubs 44
    Red Cross Cadets at Albury Park 44
Dorothy Lee - Evacuees 8
Doug Realf - Prefabs at Chestnut Way (NowThe Range) 84
Elisabeth Green & St Catherine's school – Miss Symes 53
Eric Hill
    Sketch Map of Bramley 92
    Bramley war memorial 78
    Paul Leaney and Ruth Bailey in 2006 69
Winnie Parsons - Incendiary bombs 63
Geoff Knapp & Michael Grant - Bramley ARP Wardens & Messenger Boys .. 20
Grafham and Smithbrook Women's Institute 1946 17
Hazel Mulkeirins - Bramley Women's Fellowship "War effort" 40
Herb Schuppert
    A sketch from "Army Daze" and Sergeant Caesar 59
    Canadian trooper 72
Jack Simonson - The Manitoba Dragoons Bugle Band 1942 prior to their departure for England .. 58
Jim Hook - Albert Hook and Albert Hook's grave in Salerno 77
Joan and Arthur Dunn - Their wedding in 1942. 16
John Brown
    Digging for Victory 18
    National Savings book 41
    Gas Mask 5
John Grant - Theodore John Grant and John Grant, letter from Home Guard 26
Joy Perun
    Defence Medal awarded to A.J.Edwards Smithbrook, G Company Home Guard 29
Keith Jelley - Halifax Crash at Upper Bonhurst 65
Manitoba Dragoons, Gord Sim – Regimental Badge 58
Margaret Macnamara
    Entry from Canadian soldier in her autograph book 57
    Entry from German prisoner of war from her autograph book 45
Nita Hart - Ray and Nita Oliver 11
Paul Leaney - As a young baby, passenger on the train 68
Peter Cansell - Leslie Cansell 77
Peter Elms - Street party 78
Richard Christophers - Derelict shop 42
Russell Hudson
    His father's Home Guard service certificate 25
    A message from the King 81
Ruth Bailey - A passenger on the train 68
Sally Caton – A letter to her aunt 71

INDEX

Contributors' maiden names are given in brackets where applicable.

1st Wonersh and Bramley Scout and Wolf Cubs 44
64 Platoon G Company 26
65 Platoon G Company 27
66 Platoon G Company 27
Adgey-Edgar, Captain 8
Administration & Services 34
Agriculture and Horticulture 35
Air raid shelters and sirens 21
AIRCRAFTMAN 1ST CLASS R.S.ST. RAYMOND WHITBOURN 76
ARP Wardens 20
Avery, Brian 83
B Company 25
Bailey, Ruth (Appleton) 68
Baldock, Ena (Charlton) 22,43,48
Banks, Leslie 9
Betts, Maurice 52
Blythman, Basil 21,28
Blythman, Patricia 79
Booth, Dorothy (Heaton) 48,73
Bothamley, Keith 12
Bradley, Ann (Fullerton) 45,56
Bramley C of E School 49
Bramley Juvenile Orchestra 45
Bramley Parish Council 82,84
Bramley Park 56
Bramley War Memorial 75
Bramley Wartime Police 7
British Restaurants 16
Brockman, Betty (Stevens) 15, 34, 44,51,83
Brown, John 27,41,43,82
Browne, Betty (Parsons) 38,80,84
Canadian Army 60
Cansell, Peter 64,66,77,79
CAPTAIN FREDERICK KAHL 75
Carpenter, Freda (Stevens) 9
Carter, George 73
Caton, Sally (Miles) 54,71
Chant, Jim 60
Childrens' Memories 71
Christophers, Richard 54
Civil Defence Forces 29
Comforts for the troops 43
Convalescent Home 43
Day, Avis (Turmaine) 14,16,33,37,41,76
Dig for Victory 18
Dim Out 46

Double summertime 31
Dunkirk 62
Dunn, Arthur 21,33,73
Dunn, Joan (Freer) 8,15,16,29,62
Dunsfold 61
Dunsfold Aerodrome 60
Durrant, Ivy (Whiting) 40,80
Durrant, Ralph 40
Eastwood Road 70
Elliott, Adrian 35
Elliott, David 35,36,77
Elliott, Irene 17
Excerpts from 'The Smallholding' 42
Factory Work 31
Federchuk, Joan (Sopp) 61,63
Fire Fighting 28
Fisher, Douglas 60
Freeman, Beryl (Hubbard) 14,21,31,32,37,84
Fund Raising Weeks 39
G Company 24,26
Gall, Barbara 6
Gas Masks 23
Gill, Gladys (Moore) 22,36
Gloster E28/39 64
Godalming and Farncombe Rifle Club 28
Goodwin, Joan (Nichols) 34,60
Grafham C of E School 48
Grafham War Memorial 76
Grant, Joan (Wise) 8,18,55
Grant, John 26,58
Grant, Michael 6,26,32,42,49,50
Gym and Dancing Club 44
Hampshire, Lilian (Blythman) 14,15,37,60
Harmes, Brian 79
Harms, Angela (Booker) 9,70
Harms, Brian 56,64
Harris, Bob 46
Harvey, Georgina (Formerly Mrs Turner) 29,33,71
Haygarth, Alfred 83
Hibbs, Roy 10
Hill, Bernard 5,38,50,55,62,63,71
Hill, Robin 18,21,31,49,51,63
Hill, Ron 82
Hodgson, John 22,64
Holy Trinity Church 76
Hook, Jim 25,77,83
Hooper, David 25,37,79
Hopwood, Jean (Hooper) 15,54,80
Housing Shortage 84
Hudson, Russell 25,55,70

Hutton, Mollie (Gall) 57
Identity Cards 7
Ives, John 11
Jackson, Pat 40
Jelley, Keith 64,65
Junior Activities 44
Knapp, Geoffrey 21,70
LANCE CORPORAL ALBERT HOOK 75
LANCE CORPORAL CECIL JOHN NAPPER 76
LANCE CORPORAL JOHN WILD 76
LANCE CORPORAL WALTER MILLER 76
Laws, Mike 74
Leaney, Paul 68
Lee, Dorothy (Baker) 6,8,27,29,57
Leisure 37
LIEUTENANT COMMANDER PATRICK HAVERS 75
LIEUTENANT PETER CANTI 75
LIEUTENANT-COMMANDER RALPH NORRIS 76
Lord Wandsworth College 43,48
Lord Wandsworth School 22
Lucas, Gladys (Napleton) 6,22,34
Mackenzie, Duncan 10
Mackney, John 27
Macnamara, Margaret (Blythman) 45,57
MAJOR RAYMOND BEENEY 75
Manitoba Dragoons 58,60,72
May, John 74
McEntee, Olive (Steptoe) 9
MHH 31
Mills, Maureen (Turmaine) 50
Moore, Richard 72,79
Mulkeirins, Hazel (Knapp) 23,27,57,82
Nash, Evelyn (Parsons) 18,19,36,51,62,63,73
National Salvage Drive 42
National Savings Scheme 41
News From Home 41
Oakley, Ula (Brett) 15,41,44,72
Oliver, Nita 11
Oliver, Ray 11
Other Factories 33
Parish Magazine 18,43,66,85
Peace Commemoration Plans 78
Perun, Joy (Edwards) 29,60,61,63,66
Phoney War 6
Porter, Doris (Wells) 70
PRIVATE FREDERICK WILLIAMSON 76
PRIVATE LESLIE CANSELL 75
PRIVATE SIDNEY NORTH 76
Rationing 85
Realff, Doug 6,24,82,83,84

Recycling & Salvage 42
Red Cross Cadets 44
RICHARD WOOD 76
Rogers, Elizabeth (Wison-FitzRoy) 53,61
Royal Australian Air Force 65
Rural Pie Scheme 18
SAPPER GEORGE HARBROE 75
SAPPER JAMES KINSELLA 75
School shelters 49
Schuppert, Herb 59
Searchlight Units 55
Selby-Lowndes, Guy 9
SERGEANT REGINALD DONALD ADGEY-EDGAR 75
Sim, Gord 58
Smith, Nancy (Turner) 22,44,46,49,56
Snowdenham Hall 55
South Africa 82
St Catherine's School 53
St Martha's School 54
St. Catherine's School 12
Stevens, Ray 22
Surrey Advertiser 5,17,22,23,28,37,39,40,41,43,47,52,58,79,81
Surrey Times & Weekly Press 67
Sykes, Doreen (Warnham) 33,38,43,57
Taylor, Cecily (Burges) 27,34,66
TELEGRAPHIST ALLEN HEARSEY 75
The Blitz 50,62
The Home Guard 24
The Red Cross 29
The Threat of Invasion 29
The Turning Tide 46
Thoday, Roger 83
Transport 37
Troops coming home 82
Turrell, Dick 15,35,38,58,63,64,79
Unofficial food sources 19
V1 66
VE Day 78
Victory Day 81
VJ Day 80
Waller, Christine (Longhurst) 34,46,52
Waller, Fred 15,35,48,55
War Reserve Police Force 7

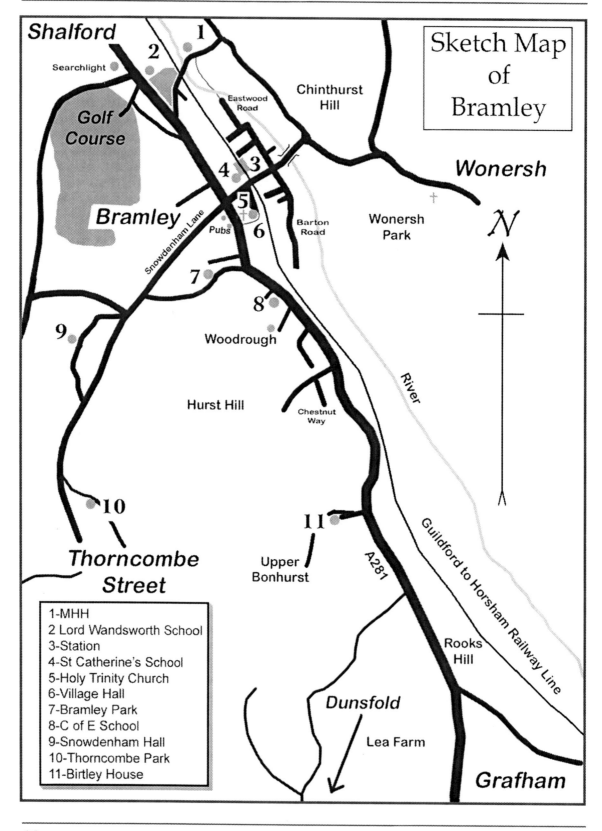

Sketch Map
of
Bramley

Shalford

2

Searchlight

Golf
Course

Bramley

Eastwood
Road

Chinthurst
Hill

1

4 3

5
6

Pubs

Snowdenham Lane

Barton
Road

Wonersh

Wonersh
Park

N

7

8

9

Woodrough

Hurst Hill

Chestnut
Way

River

10

Thorncombe
Street

11

Upper
Bonhurst

A281

Guildford to Horsham Railway Line

Rooks
Hill

Dunsfold

Lea Farm

Grafham

1-MHH
2 Lord Wandsworth School
3-Station
4-St Catherine's School
5-Holy Trinity Church
6-Village Hall
7-Bramley Park
8-C of E School
9-Snowdenham Hall
10-Thorncombe Park
11-Birtley House

d Kingdom
n\   UK Ltd.
K(9-282/A